Weather and Climate Inventory
National Park Service
Eastern Rivers and Mountains Network

Natural Resource Technical Report NPS/ERMN/NRTR—2006/006
WRCC Report 06-05

Christopher A. Davey, Kelly T. Redmond, and David B. Simeral
Western Regional Climate Center
Desert Research Institute
2215 Raggio Parkway
Reno, Nevada 89512-1095

September 2006

U.S. Department of the Interior
National Park Service
Natural Resource Program Center
Fort Collins, Colorado

The Natural Resource Publication series addresses natural resource topics that are of interest and applicability to a broad readership in the National Park Service and to others in the management of natural resources, including the scientific community, the public, and the National Park Service conservation and environmental constituencies. Manuscripts are peer-reviewed to ensure that the information is scientifically credible, technically accurate, appropriately written for the intended audience, and designed and published in a professional manner.

The Natural Resource Technical Reports series is used to disseminate the peer-reviewed results of scientific studies in the physical, biological, and social sciences for both the advancement of science and the achievement of the National Park Service's mission. The reports provide contributors with a forum for displaying comprehensive data that are often deleted from journals because of page limitations. Current examples of such reports include the results of research that addresses natural resource management issues; natural resource inventory and monitoring activities; resource assessment reports; scientific literature reviews; and peer reviewed proceedings of technical workshops, conferences, or symposia.

Views and conclusions in this report are those of the authors and do not necessarily reflect policies of the National Park Service. Mention of trade names or commercial products does not constitute endorsement or recommendation for use by the National Park Service.

Printed copies of reports in these series may be produced in a limited quantity and they are only available as long as the supply lasts. This report is also available from the Natural Resource Publications Management website (http://www.nature.nps.gov/publications/NRPM) on the Internet or by sending a request to the address on the back cover.

Please cite this publication as follows:

Davey, C. A., K. T. Redmond, and D. B. Simeral. 2006. Weather and Climate Inventory, National Park Service, Eastern Rivers and Mountains Network. Natural Resource Technical Report NPS/ERMN/NRTR— 2006/006. National Park Service, Fort Collins, Colorado.

NPS/ERMN/NRTR—2006/006, September 2006

Table of Contents

Table of Contents (continued)

Figures

Tables

Appendixes

Acronyms

AASC	American Association of State Climatologists
ACIS	Applied Climate Information System
ALPO	Allegheny Portage Railroad National Historic Site
ASOS	Automated Surface Observing System
AWOS	Automated Weather Observing System
BLM	Bureau of Land Management
BLUE	Bluestone National Scenic River
CASTNet	Clean Air Status and Trends Network
COOP	Cooperative Observer Program
CWOP	Citizen Weather Observer Program
CRN	Climate Reference Network
DEWA	Delaware Water Gap National Recreation Area
DFIR	Double-Fence Intercomparison Reference
DST	daylight savings time
DOT	Department of Transportation
DEP	Department of Environmental Protection
EPA	Environmental Protection Agency
ERMN	Eastern Rivers and Mountains Inventory and Monitoring Network
FAA	Federal Aviation Administration
FIPS	Federal Information Processing Standards
FONE	Fort Necessity National Battlefield
FRHI	Friendship Hill National Historic Site
FWS	Fish and Wildlife Service
GARI	Gauley River National Recreation Area
GMT	Greenwich Mean Time
GOES	Geostationary Operational Environmental Satellite
GPS	Global Positioning System
HCN	Historical Climate Network
I&M	NPS Inventory and Monitoring Program
IFLOWS	Integrated Flood Observing and Warning System
JOFL	Johnstown Flood National Memorial
LST	local standard time
NADP	National Atmospheric Deposition Program
NCDC	National Climatic Data Center
NERI	New River Gorge National River
NetCDF	Network Common Data Form
NOAA	National Oceanic and Atmospheric Administration
NPS	National Park Service
NRCS	Natural Resources Conservation Service
NRCS-SC	Natural Resources Conservation Service snowcourse network
NWS	National Weather Service
PASC	Pennsylvania State Climatologist office
PRISM	Parameter Regression on Independent Slopes Model
RAWS	Remote Automated Weather Station Network

RCC	regional climate center
SAO	Surface Airways Observation Network
Surfrad	Surface Radiation Budget Network
SNOTEL	Natural Resources Conservation Service Snowfall Telemetry Network
UPDE	Upper Delaware Scenic And Recreational River
USDA	U.S. Department of Agriculture
USFS	U.S. Forest Service
USGS	U.S. Geological Survey
UTC	Coordinated Universal Time
WBAN	Weather Bureau Army Navy
WMO	World Meteorological Organization
WRCC	Western Regional Climate Center

Executive Summary

Climate is a dominant factor driving the physical and ecologic processes affecting the nine park units that comprise the Eastern Rivers and Mountains Inventory and Monitoring Network (ERMN). Climate variations are responsible for short- and long-term changes in ecosystem fluxes of energy and matter and have profound effects on underlying geomorphic and biogeochemical processes. The ERMN contains significant water resources and one of the largest remaining undisturbed tracts of mixed mesophytic forests in North America. A long history of human influences in ERMN has introduced stresses on the region's natural systems, including invasive plant species, atmospheric pollutant deposition, and habitat fragmentation. Because of its influence on the ecology of ERMN park units and the surrounding areas, climate was identified as a high-priority, vital sign for ERMN, and climate is one of the 12 basic inventories to be completed for all National Park Service (NPS) Inventory and Monitoring Program (I&M) networks.

This project was initiated to inventory past and present climate monitoring efforts in ERMN. In this report, we provide the following information:

- Overview of broad-scale climatic factors and zones important to ERMN park units.
- Inventory of weather and climate station locations in and near ERMN park units relevant to the NPS I&M Program.
- Results of an inventory of metadata on each weather station, including affiliations for weather-monitoring networks, types of measurements recorded at these stations, and information about the actual measurements (length of record, etc.).
- Initial evaluation of the adequacy of coverage for existing weather stations and recommendations for improvements in monitoring weather and climate.

The ERMN climate is characterized by topographical and north-south gradients in temperature. Mean annual temperatures in ERMN generally decrease from south to north. January mean minimum temperatures in ERMN range between -5°C and -15°C. Summers in the region are warm and humid, with July mean maximum temperatures ranging between 25-30°C for ERMN park units. Precipitation is a common occurrence throughout the region, particularly during the summer months and west of the Appalachian Mountains. Mean annual precipitation for ERMN park units generally ranges from 700 to 1300 mm. Nor'easters and tropical cyclones are significant extreme storm events that occasionally impact the ERMN ecosystems. Significant positive trends in temperature and precipitation have been reported over the region. These trends are projected to continue for the foreseeable future.

Preliminary work by the Pennsylvania State Climatologist Office has identified weather/climate stations within ERMN park units, particularly those in Pennsylvania. Through an accompanying search of national databases and inquiries to NPS staff, we have identified 13 weather/climate stations within ERMN park units. These include seven stations at Delaware Water Gap National Recreation Area (DEWA), four stations at Upper Delaware Scenic and Recreational River (UPDE), and two stations at New River Gorge National River (NERI). Two of the 13 aforementioned stations are automated

RAWS (Remote Automated Weather Station) sites; one of these stations is in DEWA, while the other is in NERI. There are no manual or automated stations located at or within the remaining ERMN park units in Pennsylvania, nor are any stations located within Gauley River National Recreation Area (GARI) in West Virginia. Most ERMN park units must rely heavily on stations outside of the park units for their weather and climate data. Station coverage is most dense in Pennsylvania and for the park units along the Delaware River Valley.

Metadata and data records for most of the weather and climate stations within ERMN are sufficiently complete and of satisfactory quality. One station of interest, however, is the National Weather Service Cooperative Observer Program (COOP) station at Grays Landing, located near Friendship Hill National Historic Site (FRHI). Multiple stations have been identified having the same location coordinates as Grays Landing. The combined records of these stations go back to 1888. It is not yet clear whether these separate records are all associated with one site. Climate records from this set of stations should be used with caution.

The recent decrease in available weather observations at Johnstown Flood National Memorial (JOFL) is unfortunate, given that a primary emphasis of JOFL is to highlight a historic flood event in the area. The continuation of any climate stations that are currently active near JOFL is advised, particularly those stations with longer data records. Educational activities that are sponsored by JOFL would likely benefit greatly from this. Since there are currently no real-time weather stations in the immediate vicinity of JOFL, it could also be beneficial to partner with an automated weather station network such as RAWS to encourage the installation of a real-time station at JOFL.

Park units in ERMN generally have numerous nearby weather/climate stations. However, there are existing gaps in station coverage that could be addressed, particularly for monitoring local-scale precipitation variations. No stations are active currently in south-central DEWA. There are also no active stations in large parts of GARI and NERI. Since DEWA already has an automated station in the central portion of the park, the installation of a manual COOP station in the south-central portions of DEWA would likely suffice in helping to document local-scale precipitation patterns in DEWA. To the north, the nearest real-time observations to Upper Delaware Scenic and Recreational River (UPDE) are at least 20 km east of the park unit. Since the RAWS network already has a presence in the Delaware River Valley, we recommend that NPS pursue a RAWS installation somewhere within UPDE.

We have not been able to identify any active real-time stations in GARI and are not certain if there are any other real-time stations in the greater Gauley River watershed. It is important that the existing COOP site at Summersville Lake be retained for long-term climate monitoring near GARI. However, this site could be enhanced by adding an automated RAWS site such as those in and near BLUE and NERI. Access to near-real-time weather conditions near GARI would be useful both for managing recreational activities and for monitoring ecosystem characteristics along the Gauley River.

Acknowledgements

This work was supported and completed under Task Agreement H8R07010001 with the Great Basin Cooperative Ecosystem Studies Unit. For starters, we thank the Pennsylvania State Climatologist office in University Park, Pennsylvania, and Paul Knight in particular, for providing extensive metadata for weather and climate stations in Pennsylvania. We would like to acknowledge certain Western Regional Climate Center personnel and various National Park Service personnel associated with the Eastern Rivers and Mountains Inventory and Monitoring Network, people who played important roles in completing this report. Particular thanks are extended to Matt Marshall, Nathan Piekielek, John Gross, Margaret Beer, Grant Kelly, Heather Angeloff, and Greg McCurdy. Portions of the work also were supported by the Western Regional Climate Center under the auspices of the National Oceanic and Atmospheric Administration.

1.0. Introduction

Weather and climate are key drivers in ecosystem structure and function. Global- and regional-scale climate variations will have a tremendous impact on natural systems (Chapin et al. 1996; Schlesinger 1997; Jacobson et al. 2000; Bonan 2002). These variations influence the fundamental properties of ecologic systems, such as soil–water relationships, plant–soil processes, and nutrient cycling, as well as disturbance rates and intensity. These properties, in turn, influence the life-history strategies supported by a climatic regime (Neilson 1987).

Given the importance of climate, it is one of 12 basic inventories to be completed by the National Park Service (NPS) Inventory and Monitoring Program (I&M) network (I&M 2006). As primary environmental drivers for the other vital signs, weather and climate patterns present various practical and management consequences and implications for the NPS (Oakley et al. 2003). Most park units observe weather and climate elements as part of their overall mission. The lands under NPS stewardship provide many excellent locations for monitoring climatic conditions.

It is essential that park units within the Eastern Rivers and Mountains Inventory and Monitoring Network (ERMN) have an effective climate-monitoring system in place to track climate changes and to aid in management decisions relating to these changes. The primary objective for climate and weather monitoring in the ERMN is to "monitor key measurable climate parameters to determine rate and extent of climate trends…" (Marshall and Piekielek 2005).

The purpose of this report is to determine the current status of weather and climate monitoring within ERMN (Figure 1.1). The ERMN, which roughly follows the spine of the Appalachian Mountains, includes 9 park units (Table 1.1). In this report, we provide the following informational elements:

- Overview of broad-scale climatic factors and zones important to ERMN park units.
- Inventory of locations for all weather stations in and near ERMN park units that are relevant to the NPS I&M networks.
- Results of metadata inventory for each station, including weather-monitoring network affiliations, types of recorded measurements, and information about actual measurements (length of record, etc.).
- Initial evaluation of the adequacy of coverage for existing weather stations and recommendations for improvements in monitoring weather and climate.

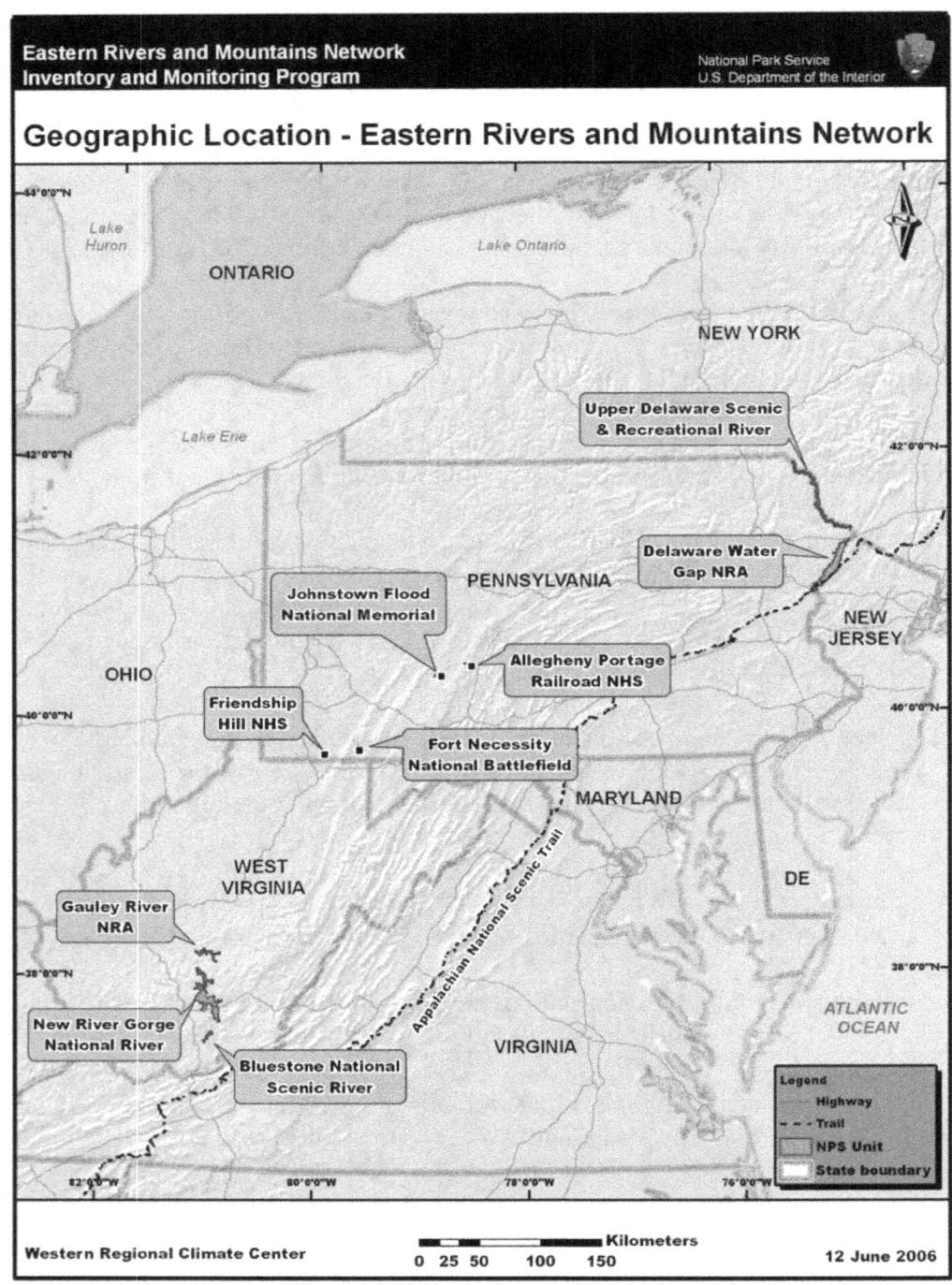

Figure 1.1. Map of the ERMN.

Table 1.1. Park units in the ERMN.

Acronym	Name
ALPO	Allegheny Portage Railroad National Historic Site
BLUE	Bluestone National Scenic River
DEWA	Delaware Water Gap National Recreation Area
FONE	Fort Necessity National Battlefield
FRHI	Friendship Hill National Historic Site
GARI	Gauley River National Recreation Area
JOFL	Johnstown Flood National Memorial
NERI	New River Gorge National River
UPDE	Upper Delaware Scenic and Recreational River

1.1. Network Terminology

Before proceeding, it is important to stress that this report discusses the idea of "networks" in two different ways. Modifiers are used to distinguish between NPS I&M networks and weather/climate station networks. See Appendix B for a full definition of these terms.

1.1.1. Weather/Climate Station Networks

Most weather and climate measurements are made not from isolated stations but from stations that are part of a network operated in support of a particular mission. The limiting case is a network of one station, where measurements are made by an interested observer or group. Larger networks usually have more and better inventory data and station-tracking procedures. Some national weather/climate networks are associated with the National Oceanic and Atmospheric Administration (NOAA), including the National Weather Service (NWS) Cooperative Observer Program (COOP). Other national networks include the interagency Remote Automated Weather Station Network (RAWS) and the U.S. Department of Agriculture/Natural Resources Conservation Service (USDA/NRCS) Snowfall Telemetry (SNOTEL) network. Usually a single agency, but sometimes a consortium of interested parties, will jointly support a particular weather/climate network.

1.1.2. NPS I&M Networks

Within the NPS, the system for monitoring various attributes in the participating park units (about 280–290 in total) is divided into 32 NPS I&M networks. These networks are collections of park units grouped together around a common theme, typically geographical.

1.2. Weather versus Climate Definitions

It is also important to distinguish whether the primary use of a given station is for weather purposes or for climate purposes. Weather station networks are intended for near-real-time usage, where the precise circumstances of a set of measurements are typically less important. In these cases, changes in exposure or other attributes over time are not as critical. Climate networks, however, are intended for long-term tracking of atmospheric conditions. Siting and exposure are critical factors for climate networks, and it is vitally important that the observational circumstances remain essentially unchanged over the duration of the station record. Some climate networks can be considered hybrids of weather/climate networks. These hybrid climate networks can supply information on a short-term "weather" time scale and a longer-term "climate" time scale.

In this report, "weather" generally refers to current (or near-real-time) atmospheric conditions, while "climate" is defined as the complete ensemble of statistical descriptors for temporal and spatial properties of atmospheric behavior (see Appendix B). Climate and weather phenomena shade gradually into each other and are ultimately inseparable.

1.3. Purpose of Measurements

Climate inventory and monitoring climate activities should be based on a set of guiding fundamental principles. Any evaluation of weather/climate monitoring programs begins with asking the following question:

- What is the purpose of weather and climate measurements?

Evaluation of past, present, or planned weather/climate monitoring activities must be based on the answer to this question. Within the context of the NPS, the following services constitute the main purposes for recording weather and climate observations:

- Provide measurements for real-time operational needs and early warnings of potential hazards (flooding, landslides, mudflows, washouts, fallen trees, plowing activities, fire conditions, aircraft and watercraft conditions, road conditions, rescue conditions, fog, restoration and remediation activities, etc.).
- Provide visitor education and aid interpretation of expected and actual conditions for visitors while they are in the park and for deciding if and when to visit the park.
- Establish engineering and design criteria for structures, roads, culverts, etc., for human comfort, safety, and economic needs.
- Consistently monitor climate over the long-term to detect changes in environmental drivers affecting ecosystems, including both gradual and sudden events.
- Provide retrospective data to understand *a posteriori* changes in flora and fauna.
- Document for posterity the physical conditions in and near the park units, including mean, extreme, and variable measurements (in time and space) for all applications.

The last three items in the preceding list are pertinent primarily to the NPS I&M networks; however, all items are important to NPS operations and management. Most of the needs in this list overlap heavily. It is often impractical to operate separate climate measuring systems that also cannot be used to meet ordinary weather needs, where there is greater emphasis on timeliness and reliability.

1.4. Design of Climate-Monitoring Programs

Determining the purposes for collecting measurements in a given weather/climate monitoring program will guide the process of identifying weather/climate stations suitable for the monitoring program. The context for making these decisions is provided in Chapter 2 where background on the ERMN climate is presented. However, this process is only one step in evaluating and designing a climate-monitoring program. This process includes the following additional steps:

- Define park- and network-specific monitoring needs and objectives.
- Identify locations and data repositories of existing and historic stations.
- Acquire existing data when necessary or practical.
- Evaluate the quality of existing data.
- Evaluate the adequacy of coverage of existing stations.
- Develop a protocol for monitoring the weather and climate, including the following:
  - o Standardized summaries and reports of weather/climate data.
  - o Data management (quality assurance and quality control, archiving, data access, etc.).
- Develop and implement a plan for installing or modifying stations, as necessary.

Throughout the design process, there are various factors that require consideration in evaluating weather and climate measurements. Many of these factors have been summarized by Dr. Tom Karl, director of the NOAA National Climatic Data Center (NCDC), and widely distributed as the "Ten Principles for Climate Monitoring" (Karl et al. 1996a; NRC 2001). These principles are presented in Appendix A, and the guidelines are embodied in many of the comments made throughout this report. The most critical factors are presented here. In addition, an overview of requirements necessary to operate a climate network is provided in Appendix C, with further discussion in Appendix E.

1.4.1. Need for Consistency

A principal goal in climate monitoring is to detect and characterize slow and sudden changes in climate through time. This is of less concern for day-to-day weather changes, but it is of paramount importance for climate variability and change. There are many ways whereby changes in techniques for making measurements, changes in instruments or their exposures, or seemingly innocuous changes in site characteristics can lead to apparent changes in climate. Safeguards must be in place to avoid these false sources of temporal "climate" variability if we are to draw correct inferences about climate behavior over time from archived measurements.

For climate monitoring, consistency through time is vital, counting at least as important as absolute accuracy. Sensors record only what is occurring at the sensor—this is all they can detect. It is the responsibility of station or station network managers to ensure that observations are representative of the spatial and temporal climate scales that we wish to record.

1.4.2. Metadata

Changes in instruments, site characteristics, and observing methodologies can lead to apparent changes in climate through time. It is therefore vital to document all factors that can bear on the interpretation of climate measurements and to update the information repeatedly through time. This information ("metadata," data about data) has its own history and set of quality-control issues that parallel those of the actual data. There is no single standard for the content of climate metadata, but a simple rule suffices:

- Observers should record all information that could be needed in the future to interpret observations correctly without benefit of the observers' personal recollections.

Such documentation includes notes, drawings, site forms, and photos, which can be of inestimable value if taken in the correct manner. That stated, it is not always clear to the metadata provider *what is important* for posterity and *what will be important* in the future. It is almost impossible to "over document" a station. Station documentation is underappreciated greatly and seldom thorough enough (especially for climate purposes). Insufficient attention to this issue often lowers the present and especially future value of otherwise useful data.

The convention followed throughout climatology is to refer to metadata as information about the measurement process, station circumstances, and data. The term "data" is reserved solely for the actual weather and climate records obtained from sensors.

1.4.3. Maintenance

Inattention to maintenance is the greatest source of failure in weather/climate stations and networks. Problems begin to occur soon after sites are deployed. A regular visit schedule must be implemented, where sites, settings (e.g., vegetation), sensors, communications, and data flow are checked routinely (once or twice a year at a minimum) and updated as necessary. Parts must be changed out for periodic recalibration or replacement. With adequate maintenance, the entire instrument suite should be replaced or completely refurbished about once every five to seven years.

Simple preventative maintenance is effective but requires much planning and skilled technical staff. Changes in technology and products require retraining and continual re-education. Travel, logistics, scheduling, and seasonal access restrictions can consume major amounts of time and budget but are absolutely necessary. Without such attention, data gradually become less credible and then often are misused or not used at all.

1.4.4. Automated versus Manual Stations

Historic stations often have depended on manual observations and many continue to operate in this mode. Manual observations frequently produce excellent data sets. Sensors and data are simple and intuitive, well tested, and relatively cheap. Manual stations have much to offer in certain circumstances and can be a source of both primary and backup data. However, methodical consistency for manual measurements is a constant challenge, especially with a mobile work force. Operating manual stations takes time and needs to be done on a regular schedule, though sometimes the routine is welcome.

Nearly all newer stations are automated. Automated stations provide better time resolution, increased (though imperfect) reliability, greater capacity for data storage, and improved accessibility to large amounts of data. The purchase cost for automated stations is higher than for manual stations. A common expectation and serious misconception is that an automated station can be deployed and left to operate on its own. In reality, automation does not eliminate the need for people but rather changes the type of person that is needed. Skilled technical personnel are needed and must be readily available, especially if live communications exist and data gaps are not wanted. Site visits are needed at least annually and spare parts must be maintained. Typical annual costs for sensors and maintenance are $1500–2500 per station.

1.4.5. Communications

With manual stations, the observer is responsible for recording and transmitting station data. Data from automated stations, however, can be transmitted quickly for access by research and operations personnel, which is a highly preferable situation. A comparison of communication systems for automated and manual stations shows that automated stations generally require additional equipment, more power, higher transmission costs, attention to sources of disruption or garbling, and backup procedures (e.g. manual downloads from data loggers).

Automated stations are capable of functioning normally without communication and retaining many months of data. At such sites, however, alerts about station problems are not possible, large gaps can accrue when accessible stations quit, and the constituencies needed to support such stations are smaller and less vocal. Two-way communications permit full recovery from disruptions, ability to reprogram data loggers remotely, and better opportunities for diagnostics and troubleshooting. In virtually all cases, two-way communications are much preferred to all other communication methods. However, two-way communications require considerations of cost, signal access, transmission rates, interference, and methods for keeping sensor and communication power loops separate. Two-way communications are frequently impossible (no service) or impractical, expensive, or power consumptive. Two-way methods (cellular, land line, radio, Internet) require smaller up-front costs as compared to other methods of communication and have variable recurrent costs, starting at zero. Satellite links work everywhere (except when blocked by trees or cliffs) and are quite reliable but are one-way and relatively slow, allow no re-transmissions, and require high up-front costs ($3–4K) but no recurrent costs. Communications technology is changing constantly and requires vigilant attention by maintenance personnel.

1.4.6. Quality Assurance and Quality Control

Quality control and quality assurance are issues at every step through the entire sequence of sensing, communication, storage, retrieval, and display of environmental data. Quality assurance is an umbrella concept that covers all data collection and processing (start-to-finish) and ensures that credible information is available to the end user. Quality control has a more limited scope and is defined by the International Standards Organization as "the operational techniques and activities that are used to satisfy quality requirements." The central problem can be better appreciated if we approach quality control in the following way.

- Quality control is the evaluation, assessment, and rehabilitation of imperfect data by utilizing other imperfect data.

The quality of the data can only decrease with time once the observation is made. The best and most effective quality control, therefore, consists in making high-quality measurements from the start and then successfully transmitting the measurements to an ingest process and storage site. Once the data are received from a monitoring station, a series of checks with increasing complexity can be applied, ranging from single-element checks (self-consistency) to multiple-element checks (inter-sensor consistency) to multiple-station/single-element checks (inter-station consistency). Suitable ancillary data (battery voltages, data ranges for all measurements, etc.) can prove extremely useful in diagnosing problems.

There is rarely a single technique in quality control procedures that will work satisfactorily for all situations. Quality-control procedures must be tailored to individual station circumstances, data access and storage methods, and climate regimes.

The fundamental issue in quality control centers on the tradeoff between falsely rejecting good data (Type I error) and falsely accepting bad data (Type II error). We cannot reduce the incidence of one type of error without increasing the incidence of the other type. In weather and climate data assessments, Type I errors are deemed far less desirable than Type II errors.

Not all observations are equal in importance. Quality-control procedures are likely to have the greatest difficulty evaluating the most extreme observations, where independent information usually must be sought and incorporated. Quality-control procedures involving more than one station usually involve a great deal of infrastructure with its own (imperfect) error-detection methods, which must be in place before a single value can be evaluated.

1.4.7. Standards

Although there is near-universal recognition of the value in systematic weather and climate measurements, these measurements will have little value unless they conform to accepted standards. There is not a single source for standards for collecting weather and climate data nor a single standard that meets all needs. Measurement standards have been developed by the American Association of State Climatologists (AASC 1985), U.S. Environmental Protection Agency (EPA 1987), World Meteorological Organization (WMO 1983; 2005), Finklin and Fischer (1990), National Wildfire Coordinating Group (2004), and the RAWS program (Bureau of Land Management [BLM] 1997). Variations to these measurement standards also have been offered by instrument makers (e.g., Tanner 1990).

1.4.8. Who Makes the Measurements?

The lands under NPS stewardship provide many excellent locations to host the monitoring of climate by the NPS or other collaborators. Most park units historically have observed weather/climate elements as part of their overall mission. An issue that frequently arises with weather/climate stations is whether to run a station and/or station network internally, using local resources, or to rely on stations that are operated by outside agencies. This will depend on the

8

needs of the individual or program that desires to obtain weather/climate data. Many weather/climate measurements come from station networks managed by other agencies, with observations taken or overseen by NPS personnel, in some cases, or by collaborators from the other agencies. National Park Service units that are small, lack sufficient resources, or lack sites presenting adequate exposure may benefit by utilizing weather/climate measurements collected from nearby stations.

2.0. Climate Background

Ecosystem processes in ERMN are strongly governed by climate characteristics (Marshall and Piekielek 2005). It is therefore essential to understand the climate characteristics of the ERMN. These characteristics are discussed in this chapter.

2.1. Climate and the ERMN Environment

The ERMN includes several parks that contain significant water resources and some of the most significant water-based recreational areas in the park system (Marshall and Piekielek 2005). In addition, the ERMN is home to a number of rare or regionally-important plant and animal species, including one of the largest remaining undisturbed tracts of mixed mesophytic forests (Mahan 2004).

Imposed on these characteristics is a long history of human uses in the ERMN region. These uses have included agriculture, logging, and mining. Urban and suburban development have also become important issues for the area (Marshall and Piekielek 2005). These human influences have introduced stresses on the natural systems in the ERMN, including invasive plant species, plant disease (Ayres and Lombardero 2000), atmospheric pollutant deposition, and habitat fragmentation (Marshall and Piekielek 2005), all of which have negative impacts on the region's biodiversity.

As a result of these stresses, the natural systems of the ERMN are likely becoming more vulnerable to damages from extreme storm events, which are a major factor in the climate of the ERMN (Marshall and Piekielek 2005). These extreme events can cause disturbances that make plant and animal communities more susceptible to diseases. They also introduce further habitat fragmentation in areas which are already significantly fragmented by human uses. Tropical cyclones, for instance, have periodically introduced large-scale disturbances into the ecosystems of the ERMN (Lugo and Scatena 1996; Lugo 2000). Riverine communities in the area are also heavily stressed by the flooding that typically accompanies these tropical systems (Lugo and Scatena 1996; Lugo 2000). During any time of the year, but particularly during the winter months, devastating flooding events can also be driven by nor'easter storms (NAST 2001). Ice storms are known to be damaging to forest communities. These events occur frequently in the eastern U.S. (Irland 2000), including the ERMN. Despite the numerous negative impacts that these extreme events can have on the natural systems of the ERMN, these events also have ecologically beneficial impacts.

Instrumental records of the climate of the eastern U.S. indicate that the region may have experienced warming over the last century (Hughes et al. 1992; Karl et al. 1996b; Karl and Knight 1998; NAST 2001), although the temperature trends for the eastern U.S. show some of the least warming throughout the U.S. (even slight cooling in southern Pennsylvania). The precipitation trends in the ERMN have shown increases over the last century, with this trend projected to continue into the future (Karl et al. 1996b; Karl and Knight 1998; NAST 2001).

These climate changes have had, and will continue to have, a marked impact on the natural systems of the ERMN. Responses of ecosystems to global warming have been postulated, and likely will vary among systems (Shaver et al. 2000). Northward shifts in the plant species comprising the ERMN forests are likely (Iverson et al. 1999; Fisher et al. 2000; Iverson and Prasad 2001). It is expected that one of the results of future climate changes in the eastern U.S. will be an increase in the number of ice storms, which can significantly disturb forest systems (NAST 2001). There may also be significant changes in the number and intensity of extreme events such as hurricanes and nor'easters (Groisman et al. 2000), all of which stress the natural systems of the ERMN.

2.2. Spatial Variability

Mean annual temperatures in the ERMN (Figure 2.1) generally decrease from south to north, with the coolest temperatures being found in southwestern New York. The Appalachian Mountains, particularly the mountains of east-central West Virginia, have cooler annual temperatures compared to the surrounding lower elevations. Mean January minimum temperatures in the ERMN (Figure 2.2) range from about -5°C near the park units in West Virginia to -15°C along the New York/Pennsylvania border, including the park units along the Delaware River. However, during winter cold snaps, temperatures can get much colder. Summers in the region are warm and humid. July mean maximum temperatures in the ERMN (Figure 2.3) are warmest in portions of West Virginia and in southeastern Pennsylvania, where mean temperature maxima are around 30°C. The ERMN park units, however, are located roughly along the spine of the Appalachian Mountains, and they have average maximum temperatures in July that are just above 25°C.

Precipitation occurs regularly throughout the ERMN network, especially west of the Appalachian Mountains (Figure 2.4). Areas such as the region around the Johnstown Flood National Memorial (JOFL) can get measurable precipitation, on average, for close to half the days of a given year. Mean annual precipitation in the ERMN generally ranges from 700 to 1300 mm (Figure 2.5). The driest locations are found in rainshadows just to the east of the Appalachian Mountains in West Virginia, throughout central Pennsylvania, and southwestern New York. Parks that lie within these drier locations include Bluestone National Scenic River (BLUE), southern portions of the New River Gorge National River (NERI), and Allegheny Portage Railroad National Historic Site (ALPO). Parks with higher precipitation include NERI and Gauley River National Recreation Area (GARI) in West Virginia; Fort Necessity National Battlefield (FONE), Friendship Hill National Historic Site (FRHI), and JOFL in southwestern Pennsylvania; and the park units along the Delaware River, including Delaware Water Gap National Recreation Area (DEWA) and Upper Delaware Scenic and Recreational River (UPDE). The highest mean annual precipitation totals by far are found in the highest elevations in the Appalachian Mountains in West Virginia, where values approach 1800 mm.

Precipitation is a common occurrence throughout the year for the ERMN (Figure 2.4). Seasonal precipitation patterns (Figure 2.6), however, show that there is generally more precipitation during the summer months.

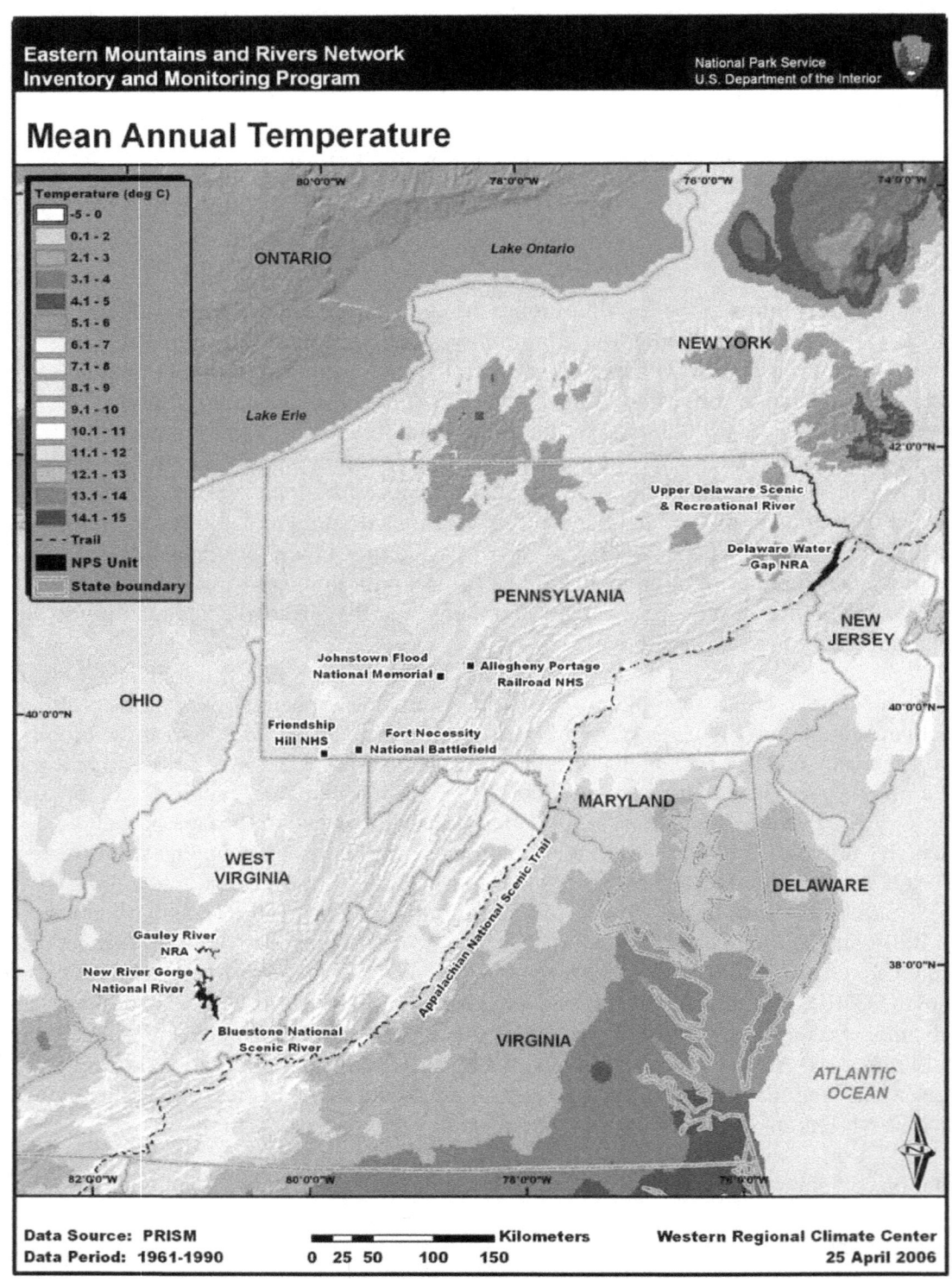

Figure 2.1. Mean annual temperature, 1961–1990, for ERMN.

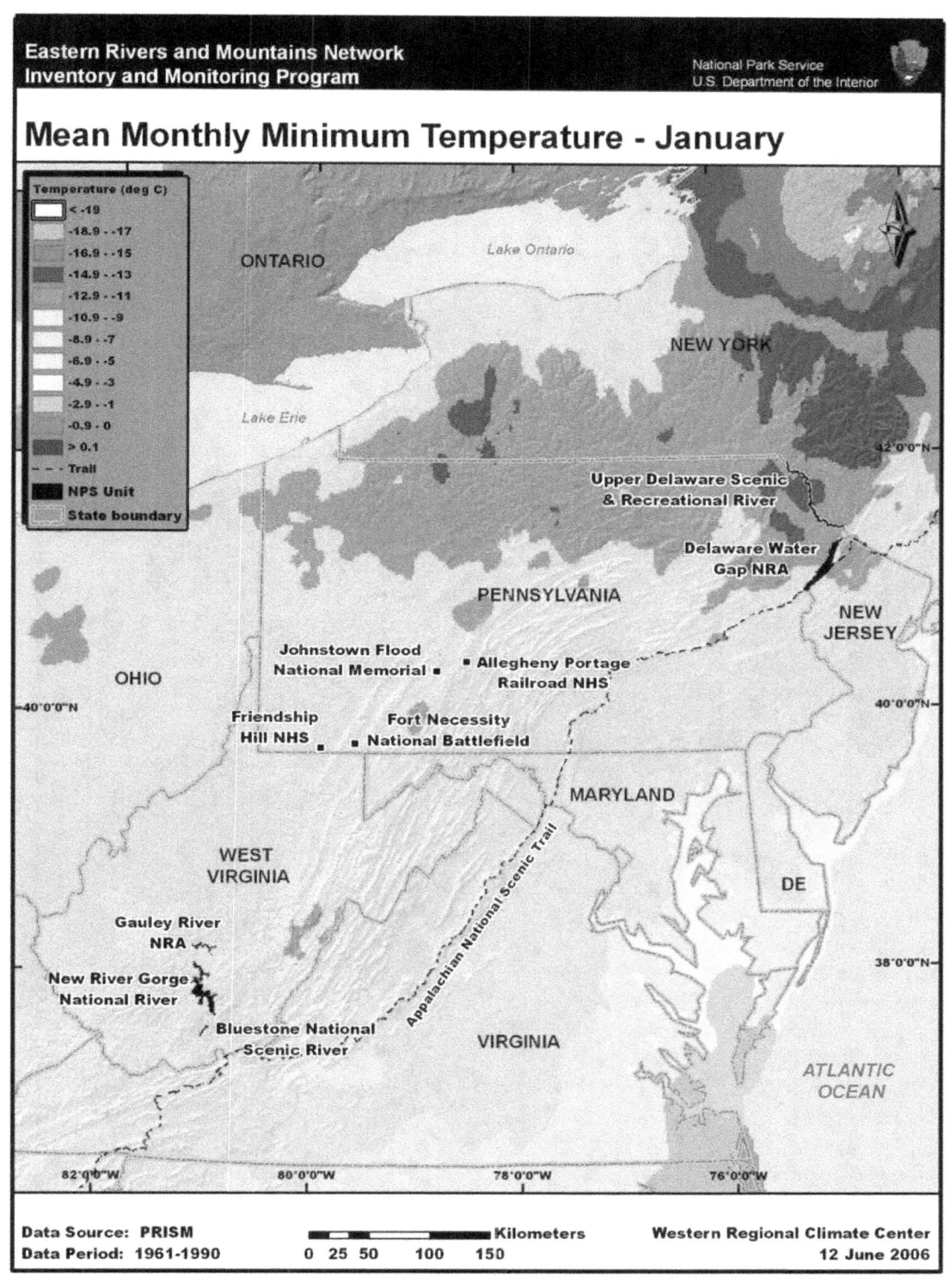

Figure 2.2. Mean January minimum temperature, 1961-1990, for ERMN.

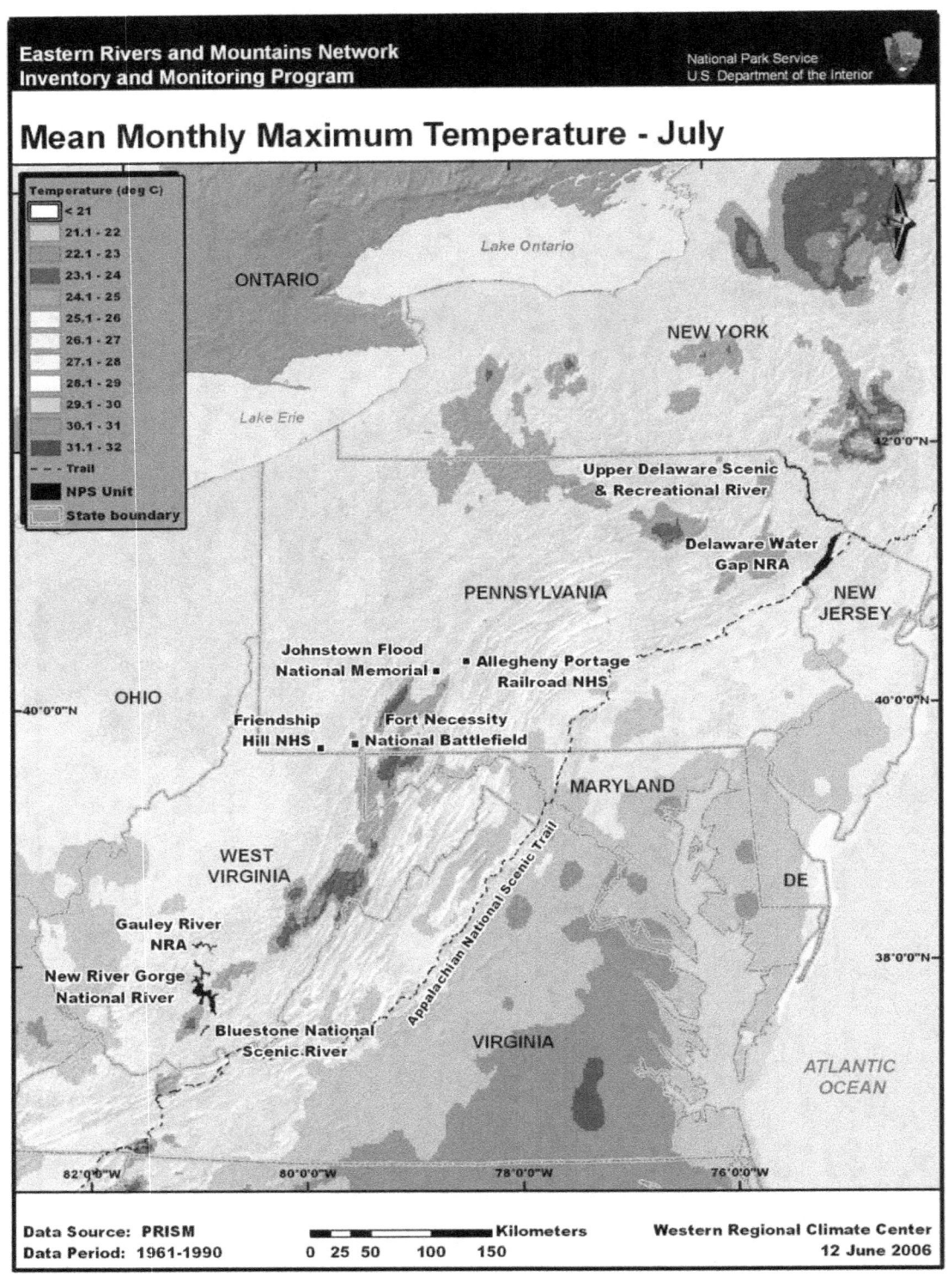

Figure 2.3. Mean July maximum temperature, 1961-1990, for ERMN.

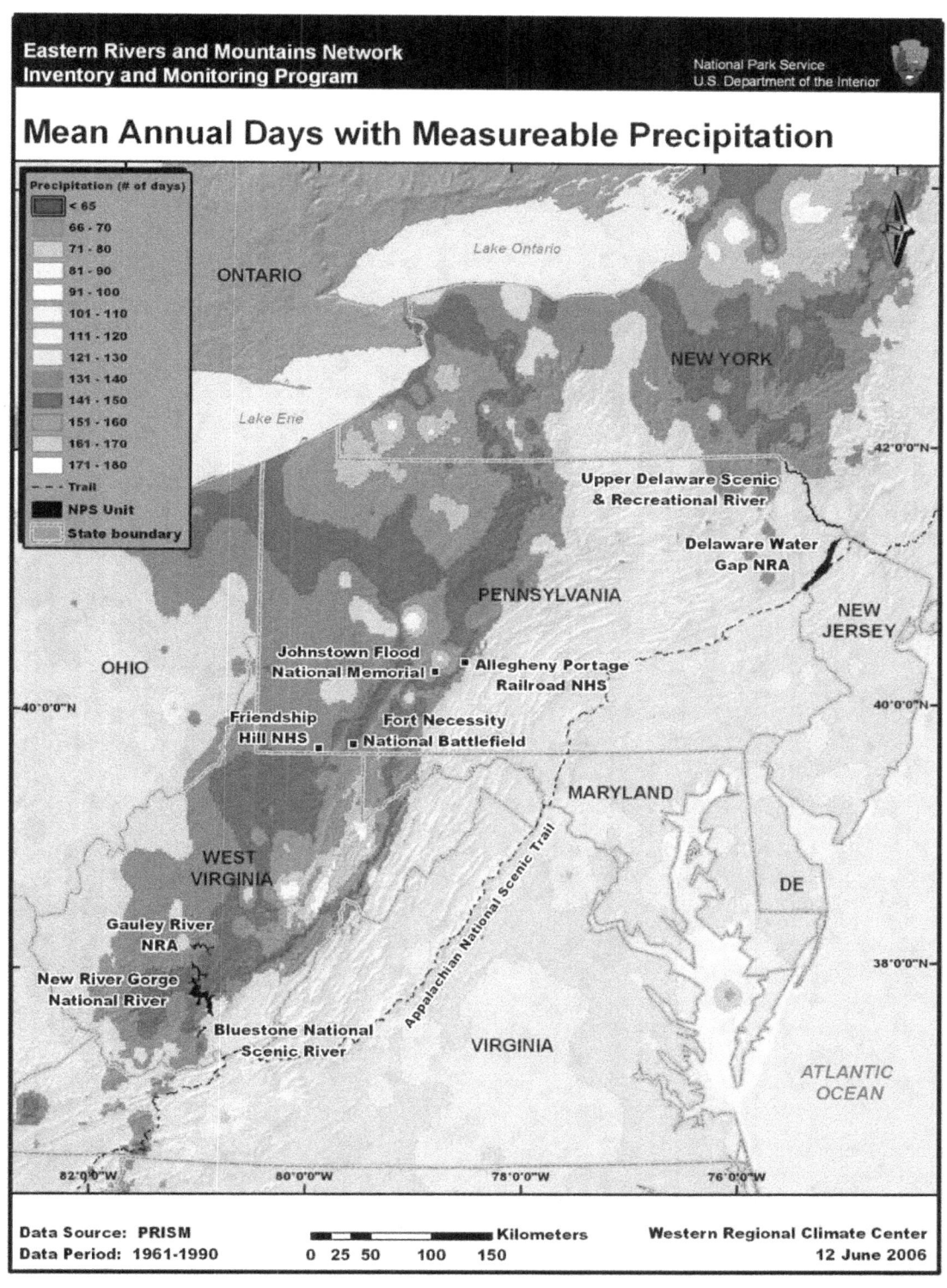

Figure 2.4. Mean number of days with measurable precipitation, 1961-1990, for ERMN.

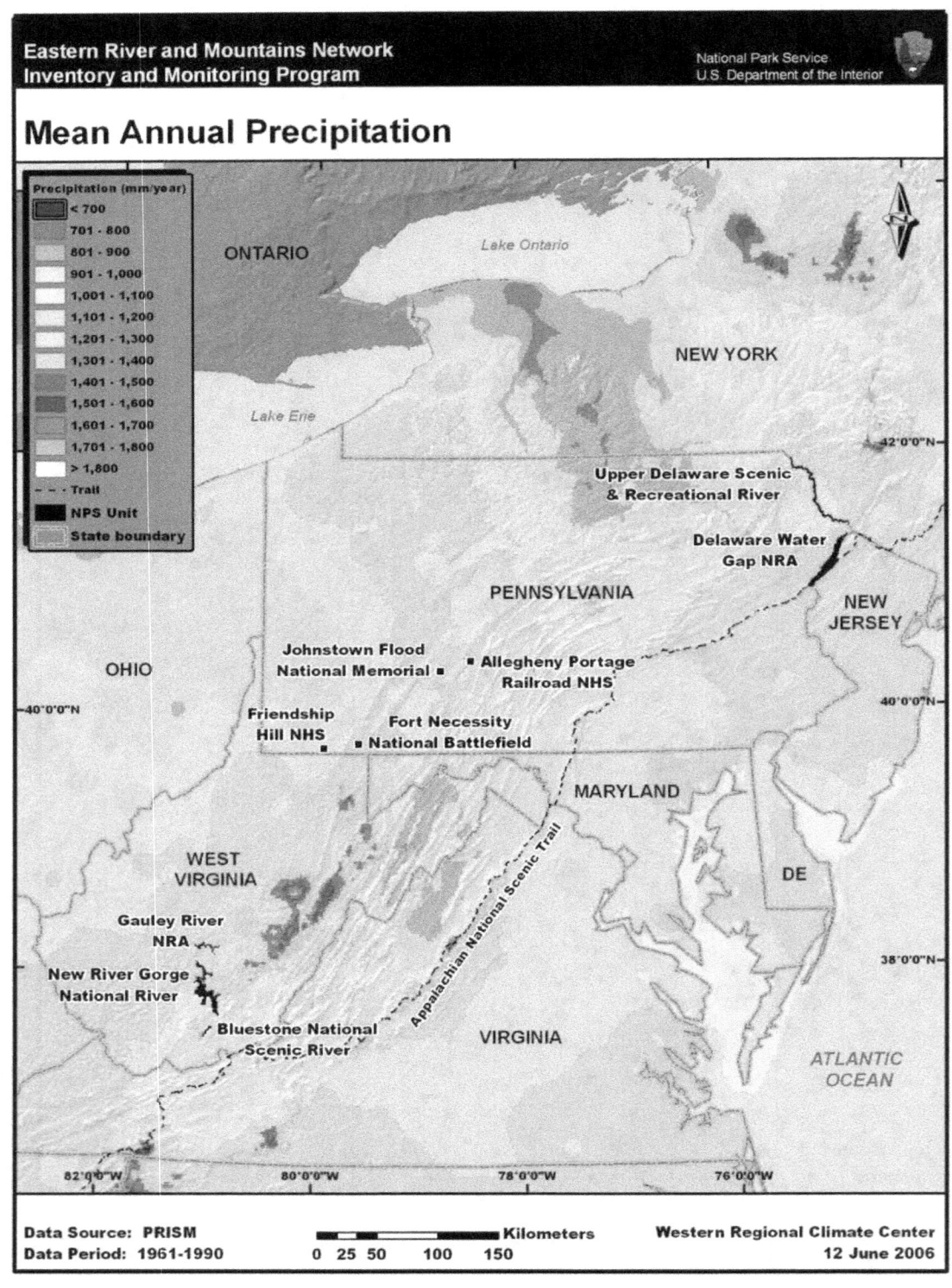

Mean Annual Precipitation

Precipitation (mm/year)
- < 700
- 701 - 800
- 801 - 900
- 901 - 1,000
- 1,001 - 1,100
- 1,101 - 1,200
- 1,201 - 1,300
- 1,301 - 1,400
- 1,401 - 1,500
- 1,501 - 1,600
- 1,601 - 1,700
- 1,701 - 1,800
- > 1,800
- – – – Trail
- NPS Unit
- State boundary

Data Source: PRISM
Data Period: 1961-1990

Kilometers
0   25 50   100   150

Western Regional Climate Center
12 June 2006

Figure 2.5. Mean annual precipitation, 1961-1990, for ERMN.

(a)

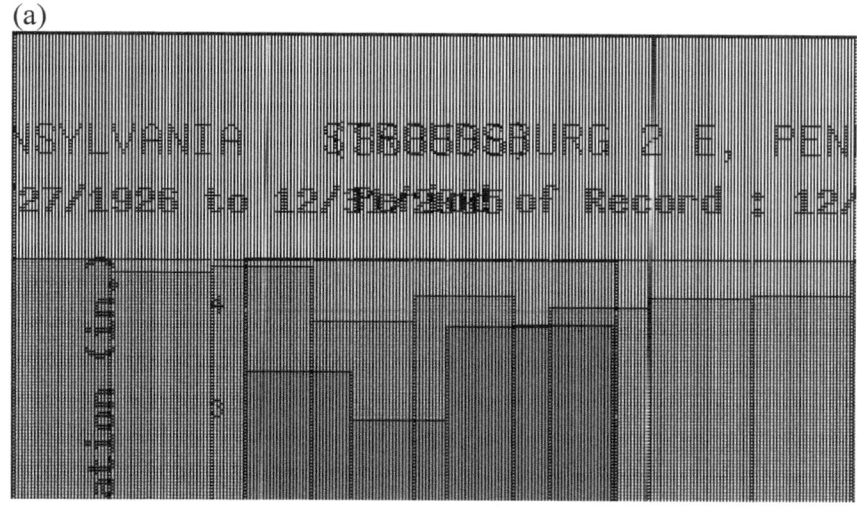

(b)

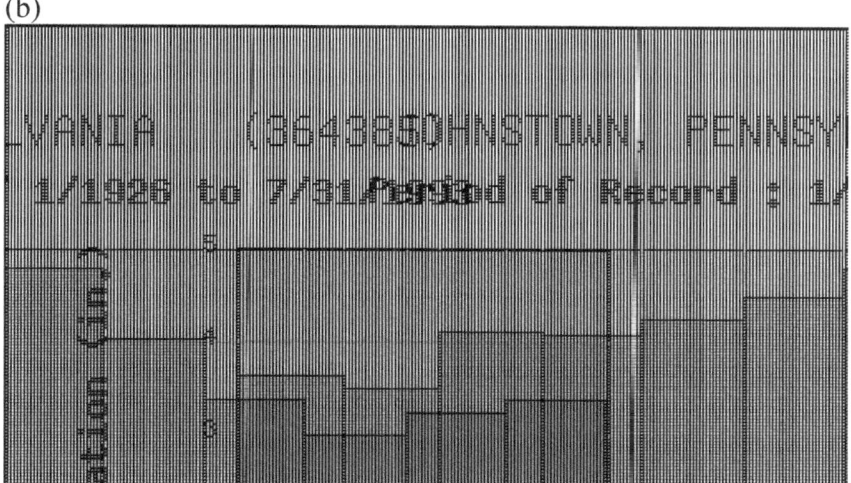

(c)

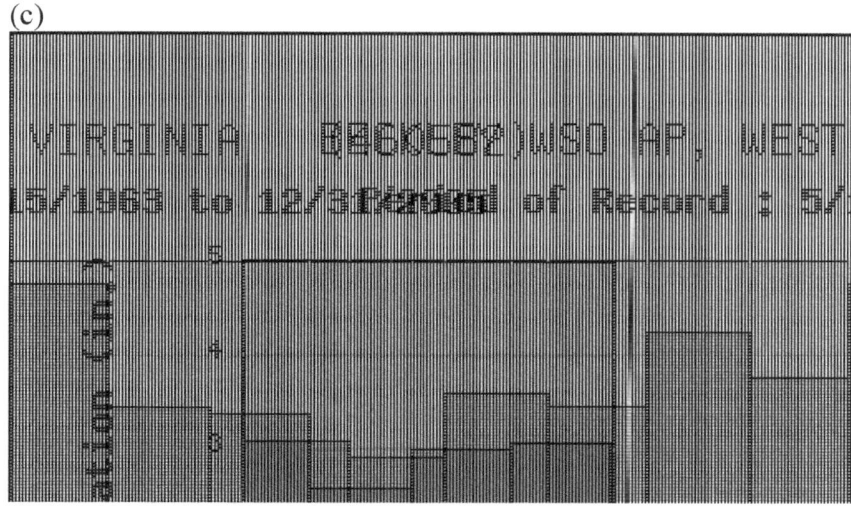

Figure 2.6. Mean monthly precipitation at selected locations in ERMN.

2.3. Temporal Variability

Precipitation in the eastern U.S. seems to have increased slightly over the last century (Karl et al. 1996b; Karl and Knight 1998; NAST 2001). In the ERMN, this is more apparent in portions of Pennsylvania (Figure 2.7) but the trends are less apparent in regions near the park units in West Virginia (Figure 2.8). Superimposed on these long-term patterns are significant droughts during the 1960s and late 1990s-early 2000s, which are apparent especially in south-central Pennsylvania (Figure 2.7).

Temporal temperature patterns for the ERMN vary markedly throughout the region. Temperatures over northern parts of the ERMN (Figure 2.9) may have risen by about 0.5°C over the last century, while temperatures in southern West Virginia (Figure 2.10) seem to be neutral or showing slight cooling during this same time period. Temperatures in the area seem to have cooled abruptly during the 1950s and 1960s. It is not clear how much of this may be due to discontinuities in temperature records at individual stations, caused by artificial changes such as stations moves. During the past 30-40 years, these temperature records show a slight but steady warming trend. These patterns highlight the emphasis on measurement consistency that is needed in order to properly detect long-term climatic changes.

Tropical cyclones are significant extreme storm events that occasionally impact the ERMN. Although some wind damage can accompany these storms, the heavy precipitation and flooding from these storms is by far a more important disturbance factor for the ERMN ecosystems. About 3 tropical storms and/or hurricanes have made landfall in the U.S. each year over the past century (Lyons 2004). Most of these storms that make landfall in the U.S. originate either in the Gulf of Mexico or the Western Caribbean (Lyons 2004). Strong hurricanes have generally made landfall in the U.S. at a rate of just under one per year over the past century (Smith 1999; Lyons 2004). The number of these storms that reach middle and northern portions of the eastern U.S. has been very sporadic during this time period but the events, when they do occur, tend to do so in clusters. These clusters of storms occur on time scales of a couple decades (Smith 1999).

2.4. Parameter Regression on Independent Slopes Model (PRISM)

The climate maps presented here were generated using the Parameter Regression on Independent Slopes Model (PRISM). This model was developed to address the extreme spatial and elevation gradients exhibited by the climate of the western United States (Daly et al. 1994; 2002; Gibson et al. 2002; Doggett et al. 2004). The maps produced through PRISM have undergone rigorous evaluation in the western United States. Originally, this model was developed to provide climate information at scales matching available land-cover maps to assist in ecologic modeling. The PRISM technique accounts for the scale-dependent effects of topography on mean values of climate elements. Elevation provides the first-order constraint for the mapped climate fields, with slope and orientation (aspect) providing second-order constraints. The model has been enhanced gradually to address inversions, coast/land gradients, and climate patterns in small-scale trapping basins. Monthly climate fields are generated by PRISM to account for seasonal variations in elevation gradients in climate elements. These monthly climate fields then can be combined into seasonal and annual climate fields. Since PRISM maps are grid maps, they do not replicate point values but rather, for a given grid cell, represent the grid-cell average of the climate variable in question at the average elevation for that cell. The model relies on observed surface and upper-air measurements to estimate spatial climate fields.

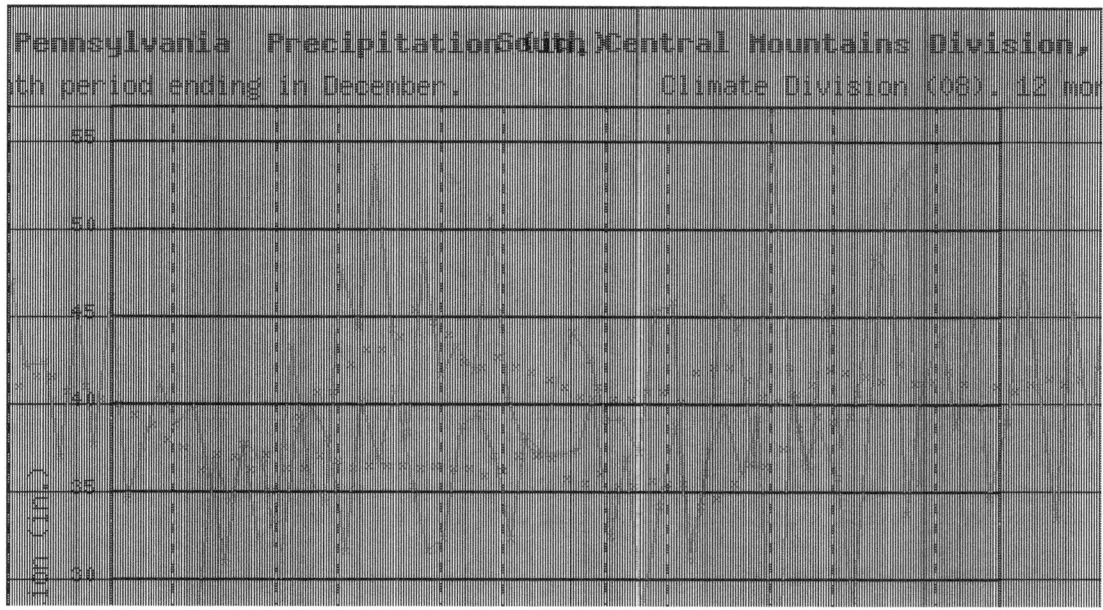

Figure 2.7. Southern Pennsylvania precipitation time series, 1895-2005. Twelve-month average precipitation ending in December (red), 10-year running mean (blue), mean (green), and plus/minus one standard deviation (green dotted line).

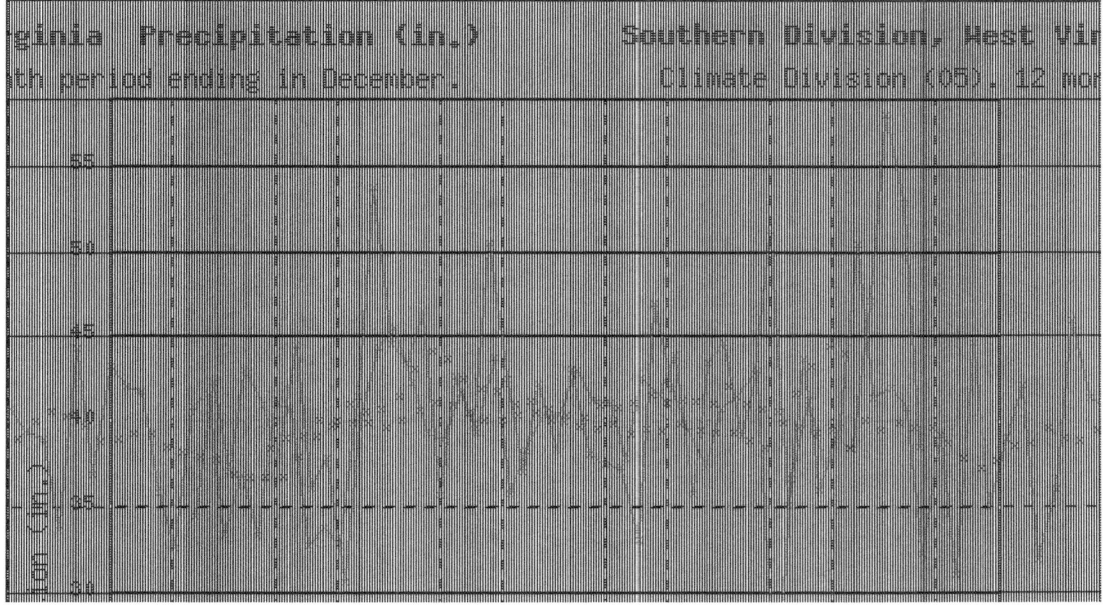

Figure 2.8. Southern West Virginia precipitation time series, 1895-2005. Twelve-month average precipitation ending in December (red), 10-year running mean (blue), mean (green), and plus/minus one standard deviation (green dotted line).

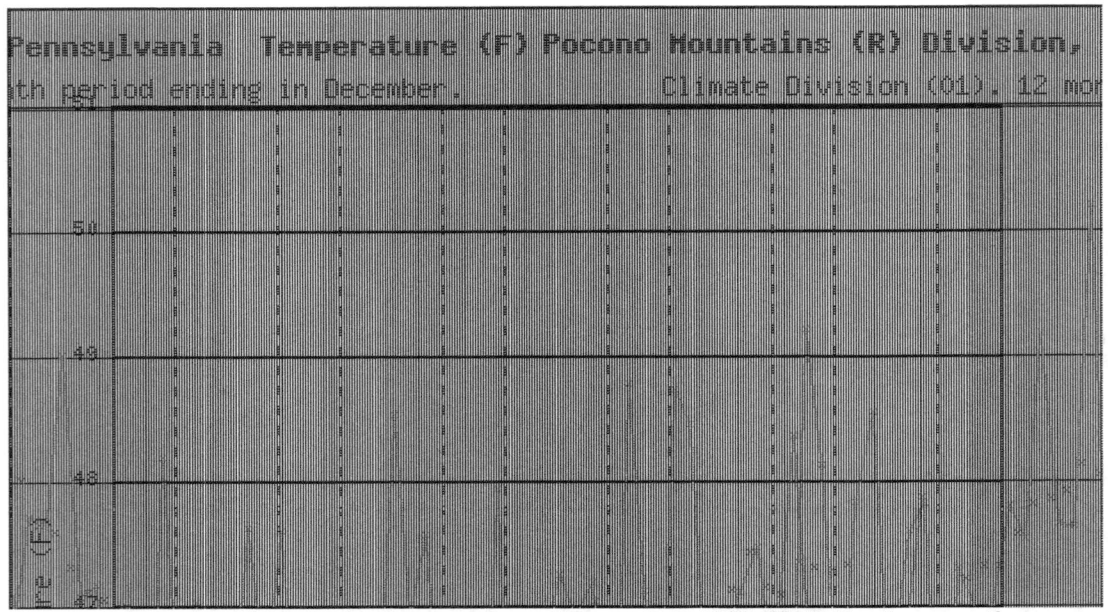

Figure 2.9. Pocono Mountains temperature time series, 1895-2005. Twelve-month average tempeature ending in December (red), 10-year running mean (blue), mean (green), and plus/minus one standard deviation (green dotted line).

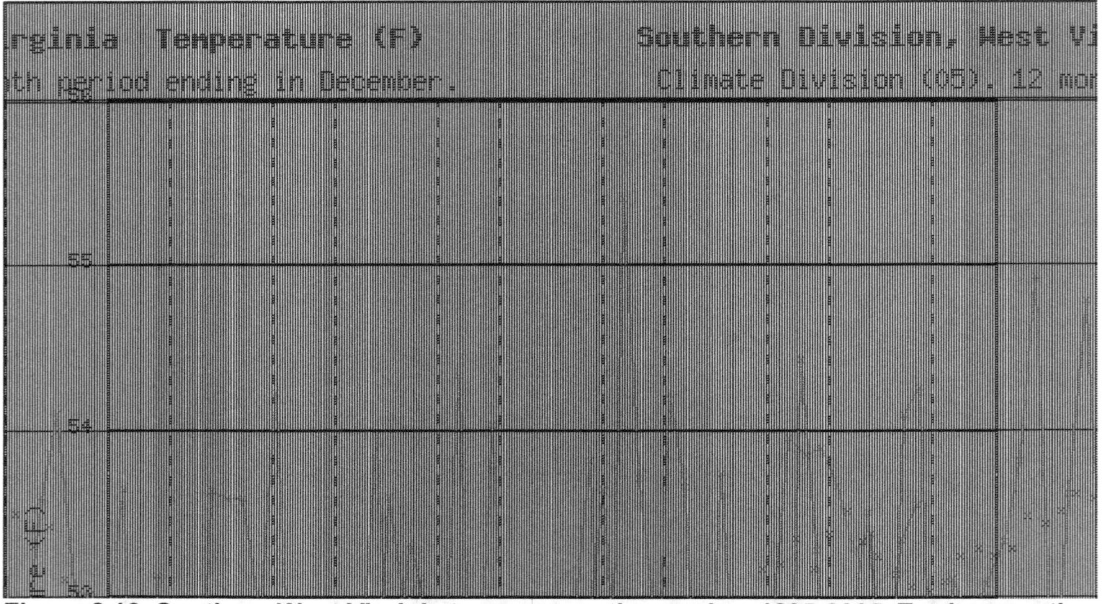

Figure 2.10. Southern West Virginia temperature time series, 1895-2005. Twelve-month average temperature ending in December (red), 10-year running mean (blue), mean (green), and plus/minus one standard deviation (green dotted line), 1895-2005.

3.0. Methods

Having discussed the climatic characteristics of ERMN, we now present the procedures that were used to obtain information for weather/climate stations within ERMN. This information was obtained from various sources, as mentioned in the following paragraphs. Retrieval of station metadata constituted a major component of this work.

3.1. Metadata Retrieval

A key component of station inventories is determining the kinds of observations that have been conducted over time, by whom, and in what manner; when each type of observation began and ended; and whether these observations are still being conducted. Metadata about the observational process (Table 3.1) generally consist of a series of vignettes that apply to time intervals and, therefore, constitute a *history* rather than a single snapshot. An expanded list of relevant metadata fields for this inventory is provided in Appendix D. This report has relied on metadata records from three sources: (a) Western Regional Climate Center (WRCC), (b) NPS personnel, and (c) other knowledgeable personnel, such as state climate office staff.

Table 3.1. Primary metadata fields for weather/climate stations within ERMN. Explanations of each field are provided as appropriate.

Metadata Field	Notes
Station name	Station name associated with network listed in "Climate Network."
Latitude	Numerical value (units: see coordinate units).
Longitude	Numerical value (units: see coordinate units).
Coordinate units	Latitude/longitude (units: decimal degrees, degree-minute-second, etc.).
Datum	Datum used as basis for coordinates: WGS 84, NAD 83, etc.
Elevation	Elevation of station above mean sea level (m).
Slope	Slope of ground surface below station (degrees).
Aspect	Azimuth that ground surface below station faces.
Climate division	NOAA climate division where station is located. Climate divisions are NOAA-specified zones sharing similar climate and hydrology characteristics.
Country	Country where station is located.
State	State where station is located.
County	County where station is located.
Weather/climate network	Primary weather/climate network the station belongs to (RAWS, Clean Air Status and Trends Network [CASTNet], etc.).
NPS unit code	Four-letter code identifying park unit where station resides.
NPS unit name	Full name of park unit.
NPS unit type	National park, national monument, etc.
UTM zone	If UTM is the only coordinate system available.
Location notes	Useful information not already included in "station narrative."
Climate variables	Temperature, precipitation, etc.
Installation date	Date of station installation.
Removal date	Date of station removal.

Metadata Field	Notes
Station photograph	Digital image of station.
Photograph date	Date photograph was taken.
Photographer	Name of person who took the photograph.
Station narrative	Anything related to general site description; may include site exposure, characteristics of surrounding vegetation, driving directions, etc.
Contact name	Name of the person involved with station operation.
Organization	Group or agency affiliation of contact person.
Contact type	Designation that identifies contact person as the station owner, observer, maintenance person, data manager, etc.
Position/job title	Official position/job title of contact person.
Address	Address of contact person.
E-mail address	E-mail address of contact person.
Phone	Phone number of contact person (and extension if available).
Contact notes	Other information needed to reach contact person.

The initial metadata sources for this report were stored at WRCC. This regional climate center acts as a working repository of many western climate records, including the main networks outlined in this section. Live and periodic ingests from all major national and western weather/climate networks are maintained at WRCC. These networks include the COOP network, Surface Airways Observation Program (SAO) networks jointly operated by NOAA and the Federal Aviation Administration (FAA), the NOAA upper-air observation network, NOAA data buoys, the RAWS network, the SNOTEL network, and various smaller networks. The WRCC is expanding its capability to ingest information from other networks as resources permit and usefulness dictates. This center has relied heavily on historic archives (in many cases supplemented with live ingests) to assess the quantity (not necessarily quality) of data available for NPS I&M network applications.

This report has relied primarily on metadata stored in the Applied Climate Information System (ACIS), a joint effort among regional climate centers (RCCs) and other NOAA entities. Metadata for ERMN weather/climate stations identified from the ACIS database are available in file "ERMN_from_ACIS.tar.gz" (see Appendix G). Historic metadata pertaining to major climate- and weather-observing systems in the U.S. are stored in ACIS where metadata are linked to the observed data. A distributed system, ACIS is synchronized among the RCCs. Mainstream software is utilized, including Postgress, Python™, and Java™ programming languages; CORBA®-compliant network software; and industry-standard, nonproprietary hardware and software. Metadata and data for all major national climate and weather networks have been entered into the ACIS database. For this project, the available metadata from many smaller networks also have been entered but in most cases the actual data have not yet been entered. Data sets are in the NetCDF (Network Common Data Form) format, but the design allows for integration with legacy systems, including non-NetCDF files (used at WRCC) and additional metadata (added for this project). The ACIS also supports a suite of products to visualize or summarize data from these data sets. National climate-monitoring maps are updated daily using the ACIS data feed. The developmental phases of ACIS have utilized metadata supplied by the NCDC and NWS with many tens of thousands of entries, screened as well as possible for duplications, mistakes, and omissions.

In addition to obtaining ERMN weather/climate station metadata from ACIS, metadata was obtained from two additional sources. First, NPS staff at the ERMN office in University Park, Pennsylvania, helped provide weather/climate station metadata information in the region for stations that were not in the ACIS database. Second, we contacted Dr. Paul Knight at the Pennsylvania State Climatologist office (PASC; Phone: 814-865-8732; Email: pgk2@psu.edu), also in University Park, Pennsylvania. The PASC office has been conducting a joint project with the ERMN to identify weather and climate stations in Pennsylvania that are relevant to the ERMN park units; PASC helped provide weather/climate station metadata information in the region for stations that were not in the ACIS database, although there is still some considerable overlap between these metadata sets. The metadata provided from the ERMN office and PASC are available in file "ERMN_NPS.tar.gz". In addition, we have relied on information supplied at various times in the past by NPS, NCDC, and NWS.

Two types of information have been used to complete the climate station inventory for ERMN.

- Station inventories: Information about operational procedures, latitude/longitude, elevation, measured elements, measurement frequency, sensor types, exposures, ground cover and vegetation, data-processing details, network, purpose, and managing individual or agency, etc.

- Data inventories: Information derived from measured data values including start and end dates, completeness, properties of data gaps, representation of missing data, flagging systems, how special circumstances are denoted in the data record, etc.

This is not a straightforward process. Extensive searches are typically required to develop historic station and data inventories. Both types of inventories frequently contain information gaps and often have built-in, unrealistic assumptions. Sources of information for these inventories frequently are difficult to recover or are undocumented and unreliable. In many cases, the actual weather/climate data available from different sources are not linked directly to metadata records. To the extent that actual data can be acquired (rather than just metadata), it is possible to cross-check these records and perform additional assessments based on the amount and completeness of the data.

Some weather/climate networks that were identified in file "ERMN_NPS.tar.gz" (Appendix G) were not included in the primary station lists for ERMN (Chapter 4). This is because the accessibility and quality of data for these networks could not be verified at the time of this report. Examples include the Integrated Flood Observing and Warning System (IFLOWS), the Citizen Weather Observer Program (CWOP), and stations run by Pennsylvania's Department of Environmental Protection (DEP) and Department of Transportation (DOT). The PASC office also has access to records of radar-estimated precipitation throughout the ERMN but particularly in Pennsylvania.

Certain types of weather/climate networks that possess any of the following attributes have also not been considered for inclusion in the inventory:

- Private networks with proprietary access and/or inability to obtain or provide sufficient metadata.
- Private weather enthusiasts (often with high-quality data) whose metadata are not available and whose data are not readily accessible.
- Unofficial observers supplying data to the NWS (lack of access to current data and historic archives; lack of metadata).
- Networks having no available historic data.
- Networks having poor-quality metadata.
- Networks having poor access to metadata.
- Real-time networks having poor access to real-time data.

Previous inventory efforts at WRCC have shown that for these weather networks, in light of the need for quality data to track weather and climate, the resources required and difficulty encountered in obtaining metadata or data are prohibitively large.

3.2. Criteria for Locating Stations

To identify stations for each park unit in ERMN, we first identified the centroid for each park unit. The centroid is defined as the average latitude and longitude of vertices defining the boundary of the park unit. We then calculated the diagonal distance of the park-unit bounding box (a box defined by the maximum and minimum latitude and longitude for the park unit). Next we identified all weather and climate stations, past and present, whose distances from the centroid were less than twice the diagonal distance of the park-unit bounding box. From these stations, we selected only those that were located in ERMN park units or within 40 km of a ERMN park-unit boundary. We selected a 40-km buffer in order to ensure the inclusion of both manual and automated stations in and near the relatively rural park units in the ERMN.

The station locator maps presented in Chapter 4 were designed to show clearly the spatial distributions of all major weather/climate station networks in ERMN. We recognize that other mapping formats may be more suitable for other specific needs.

4.0. Station Inventory

An objective of this report is to show the locations of weather/climate stations for the ERMN region in relation to the boundaries of the NPS park units within ERMN. A station does not have to be within park boundaries to provide useful data and information for a park unit.

4.1. Climate and Weather Networks

Most stations in the ERMN region are associated with at least one of four major weather/climate networks (Table 4.1). Brief descriptions of each weather/climate network are provided below (see Appendix F for greater detail).

Table 4.1. Weather/climate networks represented within ERMN.

Acronym	Name
CASTNet	Clean Air Status and Trends Network
COOP	NWS Cooperative Observer Program
RAWS	Remote Automated Weather Station Network
SAO	NWS/FAA Surface Airways Observation Network

4.1.1. Clean Air Status and Trends Network (CASTNet)

CASTNet is primarily an air-quality monitoring network managed by the EPA. Hourly weather and climate elements are measured and include temperature, wind, humidity, solar radiation, soil temperature, and sometimes soil moisture. These elements are intended to support interpretation of air-quality parameters that also are measured at CASTNet sites. Data records at CASTNet sites are generally one–two decades in length.

4.1.2. NWS Cooperative Observer Program (COOP)

The COOP network has been a foundation of the U.S. climate program for decades and continues to play an important role. Manual measurements are made by volunteers and consist of daily maximum and minimum temperatures, observation-time temperature, daily precipitation, daily snowfall, and snow depth. When blended with NWS measurements, the data set is known as SOD, or "Summary of the Day." The quality of data from COOP sites ranges from excellent to modest.

4.1.3. Remote Automated Weather Station Network (RAWS)

The RAWS network is administered through many land management agencies, particularly the BLM and the Forest Service. Hourly meteorology elements are measured and include temperature, wind, humidity, solar radiation, barometric pressure, fuel temperature, and precipitation (when temperatures are above freezing). The fire community is the primary client for RAWS data. These sites are remote and data typically are transmitted via GOES

(Geostationary Operational Environmental Satellite). Some sites operate all winter. Most data records for RAWS sites began during or after the mid-1980s.

4.1.4. NWS/FAA Surface Airways Observation Program (SAO)

These stations are located usually at major airports and military bases. Almost all SAO sites are automated. The hourly data measured at these sites include temperature, precipitation, humidity, wind, pressure, sky cover, ceiling, visibility, and current weather. Most data records begin during or after the 1940s, and these data are generally of high quality.

4.1.5. Other Networks

In addition to the major networks mentioned above, there are various networks that are operated for specific purposes by specific organizations or governmental agencies or scientific research projects. These networks could be present within ERMN but have not been identified in this report. This includes:

- NOAA upper-air stations
- National Atmospheric Deposition Program (NADP)
- U.S. Department of Energy Surface Radiation Budget Network (Surfrad)
- U.S. Geological Survey (USGS) hydrologic stations
- Park-specific-monitoring networks and stations
- Other research or project networks having many possible owners

The metadatabase files for weather/climate stations in ERMN are constantly being updated. As new weather/climate networks are identified, these will be added to the final versions of the metadatabase files accompanying this report.

4.2. Station Locations

The major weather/climate networks in ERMN (discussed in Section 4.1) have at most a few stations that are at or inside each park unit (Table 4.2). The DEWA and UPDE park units have the most weather stations both in and near park boundaries.

Table 4.2. Number of stations near (in) ERMN park units. Numbers are listed by park unit and weather/climate network.

Network	ALPO	BLUE	DEWA	FONE	FRHI	GARI	JOFL	NERI	UPDE
CASTNet	0(0)	0(0)	0(0)	1(0)	0(0)	0(0)	0(0)	0(0)	0(0)
COOP	37(0)	24(0)	76(6)	43(0)	31(0)	35(0)	40(0)	38(1)	85(4)
RAWS	0(0)	2(0)	1(1)	0(0)	0(0)	1(0)	0(0)	2(1)	1(0)
SAO	2(0)	2(0)	5(0)	2(0)	2(0)	0(0)	3(0)	1(0)	5(0)
Other	1(0)	0(0)	2(0)	3(0)	2(0)	0(0)	3(0)	0(0)	0(0)

Lists of stations have been compiled for the ERMN. A station does not have to be within the boundaries to provide useful data and information regarding the park unit in question. Some might be physically *within* the administrative or political boundaries, whereas others might be just outside, or even some distance away, but would be *nearby* in behavior and representativeness. What constitutes "useful" and "representative" are also significant questions, whose answers can vary according to application, type of element, period of record, procedural or methodological observation conventions, and the like.

4.2.1. Pennsylvania Park Units

We have identified no weather/climate stations within any of the ERMN park units located in Pennsylvania (DEWA and UPDE, while partially in PA, are considered in the next section). All of these park units have reliable COOP stations that are located nearby; however, not all of the park units have nearby stations providing reliable data in real time (e.g. JOFL; see Table 4.3 and Figure 4.1).

Although there are no weather/climate stations identified within ALPO, there are several COOP stations that are located within 10 km of ALPO (Figure 4.1). Seventeen COOP stations are currently active (Table 4.3; active stations are stations whose ending date is listed as "Present") within 40 km of ALPO; a few of these have data records extending back as far as the late 1800s. Other valuable long-term data records are found at Altoona Blair County Airport, which has both a COOP station and a SAO station. The data records for the SAO and COOP sites both go back to 1938. Upper portions of ALPO may best be represented by the COOP station at the Ebensburg sewage plant. This station has been active since 1963 (Table 4.3) and its data record is quite reliable.

No stations have been identified at or within FONE. Seventeen COOP stations are currently in operation within 40 km of FONE, along with two SAO stations and one CASTNet station (Table 4.3). The nearest station to FONE is the COOP station "Chalk Hill 2 ENE", about 4 km north of FONE. This station has operated since 1973 (Table 4.3) and has a complete data record. The nearest near-real-time observations are from the SAO station at Connellsville Airport, about 15 km northwest of FONE (Figure 4.1). This station has operated since 1989. The longest data records are available from "Uniontown 1 NE", a COOP station that has operated since 1894. The COOP and SAO stations at Morgantown Hart Field also provide useful data beginning in 1941 (Table 4.3); the data from these two sites are largely complete except for occasional gaps in the late 1990s.

Like FONE, no stations have been identified at or within FRHI. Thirteen COOP stations are currently in operation within 40 km of FRHI, along with two SAO stations (Table 4.3). The nearest station to FRHI is the COOP station "Grays Landing". This particular station has been active since 1995; however, there was a COOP station (Greensboro Lock 7) which has identical location coordinates to Grays Landing and operated from 1888-1995. It is possible that this is actually a single physical COOP site that has either had a change such as a small station move or a change in station name during its period of record. The nearest near-real-time observations are available from the SAO station "Morgantown Hart Field", discussed previously. The longest data records around FRHI are found at several COOP stations in the area that have data beginning in the late 1800s (Table 4.3).

No stations have been identified at or within JOFL. Eighteen COOP stations and one SAO station are currently in operation within 40 km of JOFL (Table 4.3). Johnstown and its immediate vicinity used to have an active SAO station and several active COOP stations (Table 4.3, Figure 4.1). However, almost all of these stations are no longer active. The nearest active COOP station is "Ferndale River", about 10 km southwest of JOFL; this station has data going back to 1979. The nearest real-time observations are obtained from the SAO station "Altoona Blair County Arpt.", which has data extending back to 1938. This airport also has a COOP station. Like the SAO station, the COOP data are available beginning in 1938; however, the completeness of this data record has only been reliable since the late 1980s. The COOP station "Hollidaysburg 2 NW" has the longest operating period in the vicinity of JOFL, having started in 1894 (Table 4.3).

Table 4.3. Weather/climate stations for ERMN park units in Pennsylvania. Stations inside park units and within 40 km of the park unit boundary are included. Each listing includes station name, location, and elevation; weather/climate network associated with station; operational start/end dates for station; and flag to indicate if station is located inside park unit boundaries.

Name	Lat.	Lon.	Elev. (m)	Network	Start	End	In Park?
Allegheny Portage Railroad National Historic Site (ALPO)							
Altoona	40.523	-78.369	390	COOP	4/13/2001	Present	NO
Altoona 3 W	40.495	-78.467	402	COOP	10/1/1967	Present	NO
Altoona Blair County Arpt.	40.300	-78.317	450	COOP	3/1/1938	Present	NO
Altoona Horseshoe Cu	40.500	-78.483	458	COOP	1/1/1893	5/16/1967	NO
Altoona Mill Run Res.	40.517	-78.450	415	COOP	9/1/1958	5/31/1977	NO
Blue Knob 2 S	40.333	-78.567	744	COOP	4/1/1975	6/7/1979	NO
Blue Knob Ski Resort	40.300	-78.583	924	COOP	6/1/1979	4/16/1984	NO
Boswell 4 N	40.208	-78.996	555	COOP	5/1/1960	Present	NO
Carrolltown 1 NNE	40.583	-78.700	634	COOP	10/1/1943	10/1/1998	NO
Coalport	40.750	-78.533	451	COOP	8/1/1943	11/30/1949	NO
Coalport 1 NW	40.757	-78.549	439	COOP	11/8/2001	1/1/2003	NO
Cresson 1 E Summit	40.467	-78.567	702	COOP	5/1/1948	4/30/1949	NO
Cresson 1 SE	40.450	-78.567	680	COOP	4/1/1965	12/31/1982	NO
Cresson 2 SE	40.450	-78.567	775	COOP	2/4/1920	4/30/1965	NO
Dunlo	40.287	-78.724	720	COOP	5/1/1948	Present	NO
Dysart 2 NW	40.646	-78.571	488	COOP	8/1/2000	3/31/2002	NO
East Conemaugh	40.346	-78.883	374	COOP	3/1/1979	Present	NO
Ebensburg	40.483	-78.717	637	COOP	8/25/1917	9/30/1963	NO
Ebensburg Sewage Plant	40.468	-78.729	591	COOP	11/1/1963	Present	NO
Ferndale River	40.283	-78.917	366	COOP	3/1/1979	Present	NO
Hollidaysburg 2 NW	40.438	-78.417	302	COOP	1/1/1894	Present	NO
Hooversville	40.150	-78.917	509	COOP	3/14/1938	4/30/1961	NO
Johnstown	40.333	-78.917	370	COOP	3/1/1892	10/28/2003	NO
Johnstown 2	40.317	-78.917	390	COOP	5/1/1948	10/28/2003	NO
Johnstown Cambria Arpt.	40.323	-78.855	692	COOP	9/1/1948	8/16/2002	NO
Martinsburg 1 SW	40.300	-78.333	415	COOP	12/1/1938	9/30/1958	NO
Mc Connellstown 4 NW	40.500	-78.133	714	COOP	10/1/1940	4/30/1950	NO
Osterburg	40.167	-78.517	351	COOP	7/1/1949	5/31/1951	NO

Name	Lat.	Lon.	Elev. (m)	Network	Start	End	In Park?
Pavia	40.267	-78.583	470	COOP	8/1/1984	Present	NO
Prince Gallitzin State Park	40.651	-78.551	463	COOP	9/1/1982	Present	NO
Saxton	40.200	-78.250	238	COOP	12/11/1940	Present	NO
Seward	40.417	-79.017	342	COOP	6/1/1938	8/31/1952	NO
Stonerstown	40.217	-78.250	250	COOP	10/1/1973	Present	NO
Strongstown	40.550	-78.917	573	COOP	5/1/1948	Present	NO
Tyrone	40.664	-78.219	271	COOP	9/1/1972	Present	NO
Williamsburg	40.467	-78.200	258	COOP	1/4/1941	Present	NO
Wolfsburg	40.042	-78.528	361	COOP	7/1/1950	Present	NO
Altoona Blair County Arpt.	40.300	-78.317	450	SAO	3/1/1938	Present	NO
Johnstown Cambria Arpt.	40.323	-78.855	692	SAO	9/1/1948	8/16/2002	NO
Cresson	40.450	-78.617	689	WBAN	12/1/1931	3/31/1937	NO

Fort Necessity National Battlefield (FONE)

Name	Lat.	Lon.	Elev. (m)	Network	Start	End	In Park?
Laurel Hill State Park	39.988	-79.251	615	CASTNet	12/1/1987	Present	NO
Albright	39.479	-79.628	372	COOP	5/1/1953	Present	NO
Bittinger 2 NW	39.617	-79.250	824	COOP	5/1/1953	3/31/1976	NO
Brandonville	39.667	-79.617	548	COOP	5/1/1909	7/1/1989	NO
Chalk Hill 2 ENE	39.851	-79.583	604	COOP	10/1/1973	Present	NO
Confluence 1 NW	39.833	-79.367	406	COOP	4/1/1892	9/2/2002	NO
Confluence 1 SW Dam	39.799	-79.367	454	COOP	7/1/1946	Present	NO
Connellsville	40.017	-79.600	265	COOP	10/1/1928	9/22/1998	NO
Connellsville 2 E	40.017	-79.550	397	COOP	5/1/1948	9/30/1964	NO
Connellsville 2 SSW	39.997	-79.596	274	COOP	9/1/1964	Present	NO
Connellsville 3	40.000	-79.583	323	COOP	3/1/1971	8/1/1971	NO
Coopers Rock St. Forest	39.677	-79.772	695	COOP	1/1/1978	Present	NO
Donegal 2 NW	40.133	-79.400	548	COOP	9/1/1943	Present	NO
Friendsville	39.617	-79.467	698	COOP	8/1/1948	9/30/1950	NO
Friendsville	39.667	-79.400	461	COOP	9/1/1950	7/31/1952	NO
Friendsville 2 W	39.667	-79.450	610	COOP	10/1/1919	7/31/1953	NO
Grantsville	39.700	-79.150	726	COOP	1/1/1895	9/30/1971	NO
Grays Landing	39.783	-79.917	244	COOP	9/1/1995	Present	NO
Green Lick Reservoir	40.100	-79.500	360	COOP	2/1/1977	3/31/1978	NO
Greensboro Lock 7	39.783	-79.917	240	COOP	10/1/1888	9/27/1995	NO
Greensboro Lock 7 Upper	39.783	-79.917	247	COOP	6/1/1948	12/31/1948	NO
Kingwood	39.467	-79.683	567	COOP	5/7/1889	11/30/1948	NO
Lake Lynn	39.720	-79.856	274	COOP	4/1/1928	Present	NO
Mc Henry 2 NW	39.583	-79.367	817	COOP	10/1/1970	12/1/1993	NO
Morgantown 1	39.633	-79.950	320	COOP	5/1/1872	5/31/1952	NO
Morgantown Hart Field	39.643	-79.916	378	COOP	4/1/1941	Present	NO
Morgantown Lock & Dam	39.617	-79.967	252	COOP	9/1/1921	Present	NO
Morgantown Lock 1 U	39.633	-79.967	253	COOP	8/1/1948	12/31/1948	NO
Mount Davis	39.800	-79.188	832	COOP	5/31/1996	Present	NO
Mount Pleasant	40.216	-79.499	306	COOP	2/1/1981	Present	NO
Mount Pleasant 6 SE	40.100	-79.433	595	COOP	3/1/1978	12/31/1980	NO
New Stanton 1 SW	40.200	-79.633	290	COOP	3/1/1952	Present	NO
Newell	40.083	-79.900	247	COOP	10/1/1901	12/31/1980	NO

Name	Lat.	Lon.	Elev. (m)	Network	Start	End	In Park?
Point Marion Lock 8	39.733	-79.917	247	COOP	6/1/1951	Present	NO
Reedsville Exp Farm	39.500	-79.833	537	COOP	4/1/1965	3/31/1978	NO
Rices Landing L 6	39.950	-80.000	238	COOP	7/1/1943	10/27/1965	NO
Rices Landing L 6 Upper	39.950	-80.000	238	COOP	6/1/1948	12/31/1948	NO
Seven Springs	40.017	-79.300	866	COOP	9/7/1982	2/1/1995	NO
Sines Deep Creek	39.524	-79.412	622	COOP	8/1/1928	Present	NO
Sines Deep Creek 2	39.533	-79.417	622	COOP	5/1/1963	1/1/1970	NO
Springs 1 SW	39.733	-79.167	763	COOP	2/1/1917	11/30/1958	NO
Terra Alta	39.450	-79.550	790	COOP	8/1/1948	3/28/1970	NO
Terra Alta No 1	39.447	-79.547	802	COOP	8/1/1948	Present	NO
Uniontown 1 NE	39.915	-79.719	291	COOP	1/1/1894	Present	NO
Connellsville Airport	39.959	-79.657	386	SAO	8/1/1989	Present	NO
Morgantown Hart Field	39.643	-79.916	378	SAO	4/1/1941	Present	NO
Connellsville AAF	39.950	-79.650	384	WBAN	10/1/1941	1/31/1946	NO
Keyser Ridge	39.700	-79.250	878	WBAN	2/1/1931	12/31/1935	NO
Uniontown Burgess AAF	39.833	-79.667	363	WBAN	3/1/1926	8/31/1936	NO

Friendship Hill National Historic Site (FRHI)

Name	Lat.	Lon.	Elev. (m)	Network	Start	End	In Park?
Albright	39.479	-79.628	372	COOP	5/1/1953	Present	NO
Brandonville	39.667	-79.617	548	COOP	5/1/1909	7/1/1989	NO
Chalk Hill 2 ENE	39.851	-79.583	604	COOP	10/1/1973	Present	NO
Charleroi	40.133	-79.917	317	COOP	5/1/1948	8/1/2005	NO
Charleroi Lock 4	40.150	-79.900	228	COOP	1/1/1931	Present	NO
Charleroi Lock 4 Upper	40.150	-79.917	226	COOP	6/1/1948	12/31/1948	NO
Connellsville	40.017	-79.600	265	COOP	10/1/1928	9/22/1998	NO
Connellsville 2 E	40.017	-79.550	397	COOP	5/1/1948	9/30/1964	NO
Connellsville 2 SSW	39.997	-79.596	274	COOP	9/1/1964	Present	NO
Connellsville 3	40.000	-79.583	323	COOP	3/1/1971	8/1/1971	NO
Coopers Rock State Forest	39.677	-79.772	695	COOP	1/1/1978	Present	NO
Fairmont	39.467	-80.133	396	COOP	2/3/1892	Present	NO
Grays Landing	39.783	-79.917	244	COOP	9/1/1995	Present	NO
Greensboro Lock 7	39.783	-79.917	240	COOP	10/1/1888	9/27/1995	NO
Greensboro Lock 7 Upper	39.783	-79.917	247	COOP	6/1/1948	12/31/1948	NO
Hoult Lock 15	39.500	-80.133	268	COOP	9/1/1921	8/18/1967	NO
Hoult Lock 15 Upper	39.567	-80.133	268	COOP	8/1/1948	12/31/1948	NO
Kingwood	39.467	-79.683	567	COOP	5/7/1889	11/30/1948	NO
Lake Lynn	39.720	-79.856	274	COOP	4/1/1928	Present	NO
Morgantown 1	39.633	-79.950	320	COOP	5/1/1872	5/31/1952	NO
Morgantown Hart Field	39.643	-79.916	378	COOP	4/1/1941	Present	NO
Morgantown Lock & Dam	39.617	-79.967	252	COOP	9/1/1921	Present	NO
Morgantown Lock 1 U	39.633	-79.967	253	COOP	8/1/1948	12/31/1948	NO
Newell	40.083	-79.900	247	COOP	10/1/1901	12/31/1980	NO
Point Marion Lock 8	39.733	-79.917	247	COOP	6/1/1951	Present	NO
Reedsville Exp Farm	39.500	-79.833	537	COOP	4/1/1965	3/31/1978	NO
Rices Landing L 6	39.950	-80.000	238	COOP	7/1/1943	10/27/1965	NO
Rices Landing L 6 Upper	39.950	-80.000	238	COOP	6/1/1948	12/31/1948	NO
Uniontown 1 NE	39.915	-79.719	291	COOP	1/1/1894	Present	NO

Name	Lat.	Lon.	Elev. (m)	Network	Start	End	In Park?
Waynesburg 1 E	39.900	-80.167	287	COOP	5/1/1948	Present	NO
Waynesburg 2 W	39.900	-80.217	299	COOP	3/14/1921	5/31/1962	NO
Connellsville Airport	39.959	-79.657	386	SAO	8/1/1989	Present	NO
Morgantown Hart Field	39.643	-79.916	378	SAO	4/1/1941	Present	NO
Connellsville AAF	39.950	-79.650	384	WBAN	10/1/1941	1/31/1946	NO
Uniontown Burgess AAF	39.833	-79.667	363	WBAN	3/1/1926	8/31/1936	NO
Johnstown Flood National Memorial (JOFL)							
Altoona	40.523	-78.369	390	COOP	4/1/2001	Present	NO
Altoona 3 W	40.495	-78.467	402	COOP	5/1/1967	Present	NO
Altoona Blair County Arpt.	40.300	-78.317	450	COOP	3/1/1938	Present	NO
Altoona Horseshoe Cu	40.500	-78.483	458	COOP	1/1/1893	5/16/1967	NO
Altoona Mill Run Res.	40.517	-78.450	415	COOP	9/1/1958	5/31/1977	NO
Blairsville 5 E	40.433	-79.150	616	COOP	4/1/1935	7/22/1978	NO
Blairsville 5 E 2	40.433	-79.183	567	COOP	7/22/1978	11/3/1988	NO
Blue Knob 2 S	40.333	-78.567	744	COOP	4/1/1975	6/7/1979	NO
Blue Knob Ski Resort	40.300	-78.583	924	COOP	6/1/1979	4/16/1984	NO
Boswell 4 N	40.208	-78.996	555	COOP	5/1/1960	Present	NO
Boswell 6 WNW	40.167	-79.133	784	COOP	12/12/1942	5/31/1960	NO
Buckstown 1 SE	40.063	-78.842	750	COOP	6/1/1943	Present	NO
Carrolltown 1 NNE	40.583	-78.700	634	COOP	10/1/1943	10/1/1998	NO
Cresson 1 E Summit	40.467	-78.567	702	COOP	5/1/1948	4/30/1949	NO
Cresson 1 SE	40.450	-78.567	680	COOP	4/1/1965	12/31/1982	NO
Cresson 2 SE	40.450	-78.567	775	COOP	2/4/1920	4/30/1965	NO
Dunlo	40.287	-78.724	720	COOP	5/1/1948	Present	NO
Dysart 2 NW	40.646	-78.571	488	COOP	8/1/2000	3/31/2002	NO
East Conemaugh	40.346	-78.883	374	COOP	3/1/1979	Present	NO
Ebensburg	40.483	-78.717	637	COOP	8/25/1917	9/30/1963	NO
Ebensburg Sewage Plant	40.468	-78.729	591	COOP	11/1/1963	Present	NO
Ferndale River	40.283	-78.917	366	COOP	3/1/1979	Present	NO
Hollidaysburg 2 NW	40.438	-78.417	302	COOP	1/1/1894	Present	NO
Hooversville	40.150	-78.917	509	COOP	3/14/1938	4/30/1961	NO
Indiana 3 SE	40.600	-79.117	336	COOP	10/1/1946	Present	NO
Johnstown	40.333	-78.917	370	COOP	3/1/1892	10/28/2003	NO
Johnstown 2	40.317	-78.917	390	COOP	5/1/1948	10/28/2003	NO
Johnstown Cambria Arpt.	40.323	-78.855	692	COOP	9/1/1948	8/16/2002	NO
Kegg	39.983	-78.717	390	COOP	3/1/1951	10/1/1991	NO
Laurel Mountain	40.200	-79.188	841	COOP	10/1/1970	Present	NO
Laurel Summit	40.169	-79.141	832	COOP	4/1/1997	Present	NO
Martinsburg 1 SW	40.300	-78.333	415	COOP	12/1/1938	9/30/1958	NO
Osterburg	40.167	-78.517	351	COOP	7/1/1949	5/31/1951	NO
Pavia	40.267	-78.583	470	COOP	8/1/1984	Present	NO
Prince Gallitzin St. Park	40.651	-78.551	463	COOP	9/1/1982	Present	NO
Seward	40.417	-79.017	342	COOP	6/1/1938	8/31/1952	NO
Shawnee State Park	40.033	-78.637	389	COOP	7/1/1991	Present	NO
Stoystown	40.100	-78.950	549	COOP	4/1/1961	7/1/1992	NO
Strongstown	40.550	-78.917	573	COOP	5/1/1948	Present	NO

Name	Lat.	Lon.	Elev. (m)	Network	Start	End	In Park?
Wolfsburg	40.042	-78.528	361	COOP	7/1/1950	Present	NO
Altoona Blair County Arpt.	40.300	-78.317	450	SAO	3/1/1938	Present	NO
Blairsville 5 E	40.433	-79.150	616	SAO	4/1/1935	7/22/1978	NO
Johnstown Cambria Arpt.	40.323	-78.855	692	SAO	9/1/1948	8/16/2002	NO
Boswell	40.183	-79.133	818	WBAN	11/1/1934	9/30/1948	NO
Buckstown	40.067	-78.833	758	WBAN	11/1/1930	1/31/1945	NO
Cresson	40.450	-78.617	689	WBAN	12/1/1931	3/31/1937	NO

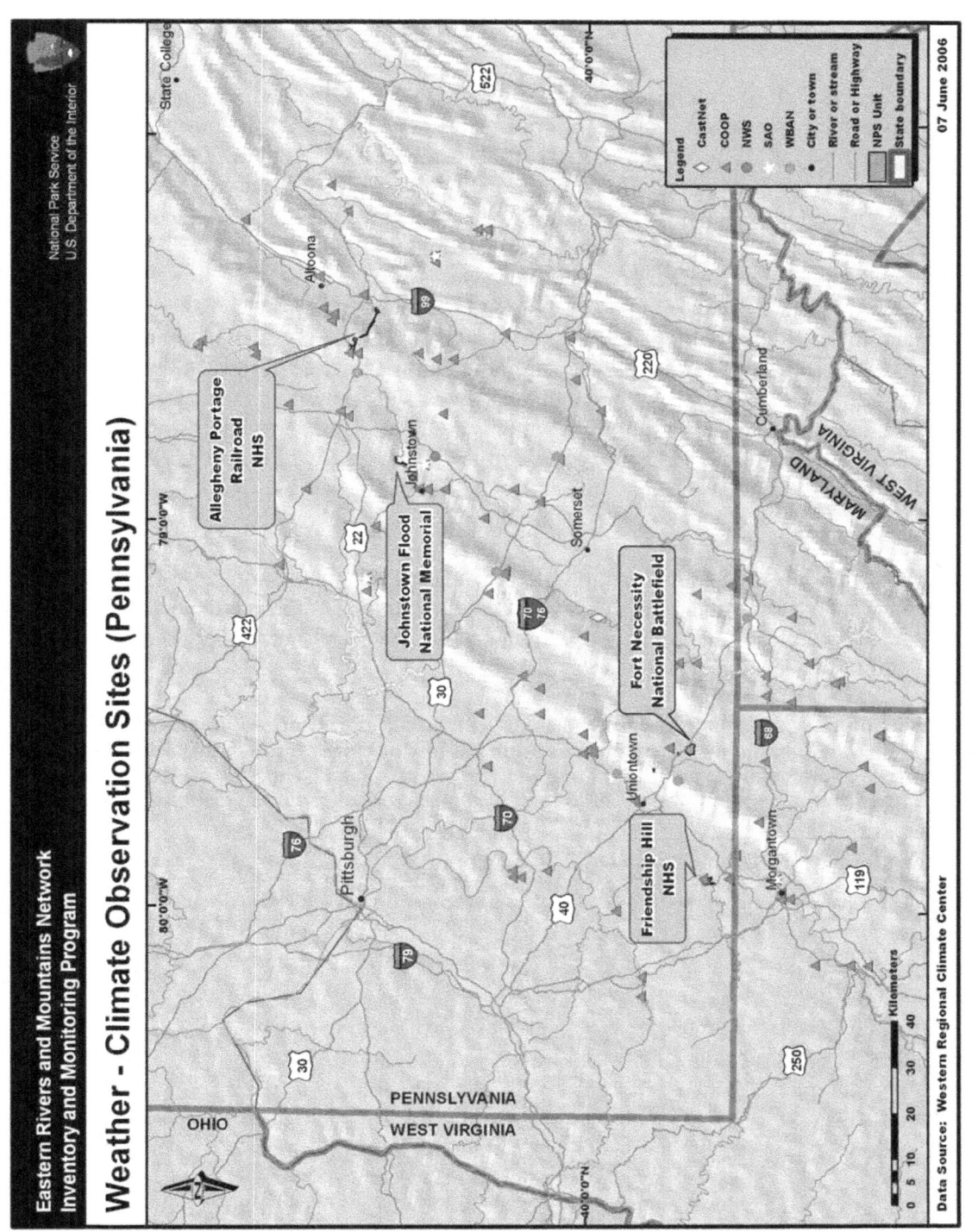

Figure 4.1. Station locations for ERMN park units in Pennsylvania. Some COOP sites are co-labeled as NWS or WBAN.

33

4.2.2. Tri-State Park Units

There are several active and historical weather/climate stations located within DEWA (Table 4.4). These stations are located either in the northern half or the very southernmost part of DEWA (Figure 4.2). The only active sites in DEWA are a COOP station at the southern edge of DEWA (Columbia 2 N), which has operated since 1971, and a RAWS station (Loch Lomond), active since 2004.

There are 31 active COOP stations and five active SAO stations located within 40 km of DEWA, including those stations located inside park boundaries (Table 4.4). Of the five SAO stations that have been identified for DEWA, four of these are less than 20 km outside of DEWA (Figure 4.2). The SAO station "Tobyhanna Pocono Mtn. AP" has the longest data record of the five SAO stations, going back to 1934. The other four SAO stations have data records that are each 30 years or less in length (Table 4.4). Several COOP stations in the vicinity of DEWA also provide longer data records, some of which go back to the 1800s.

The stations within UPDE are all COOP stations (Figure 4.2, Table 4.4). There are four such stations in UPDE, scattered along the Delaware River Valley. Three of these COOP stations are still active and they all have data records that are 50 years or more in length. However, there are concerns with two of these sites. Data from Milanville have not been reliable since 1975 and must be treated with caution. The data record for the COOP station "Equinunk 2 NW" is very complete but the station only measures precipitation. There are several COOP stations within 40 km of UPDE that have operated since the late 1800s.

There are no real-time weather stations in UPDE. The closest such stations to UPDE are the Loch Lomond RAWS station in DEWA, about 20 km from the southern edge of UPDE, and the SAO station "Monticello Sullivan", about 20 km east of DEWA (Figure 4.2). The data record for this SAO station goes back to 1969 (Table 4.4).

Table 4.4. Weather/climate stations for ERMN park units in the Tri-State region. Stations inside park units and within 40 km of the park unit boundary are included. Each listing includes station name, location, and elevation; weather/climate network associated with station; operational start/end dates for station; and flag to indicate if station is located inside park unit boundaries.

Name	Lat.	Lon.	Elev. (m)	Network	Start	End	In Park?
Delaware Water Gap National Recreation Area (DEWA)							
Columbia 2 N	40.971	-75.118	110	COOP	8/1/1971	Present	YES
Dingmans Ferry	41.217	-74.867	131	COOP	11/6/1939	12/8/1982	YES
Layton 2	41.250	-74.867	122	COOP	4/1/1962	2/12/1973	YES
Layton 3 NW	41.250	-74.850	143	COOP	6/1/1900	2/28/1973	YES
Montague Milford	41.300	-74.800	113	COOP	11/5/1956	6/8/2004	YES
Tocks Island	41.017	-75.083	88	COOP	6/1/1967	2/1/1999	YES
Loch Lomond	41.204	-74.890	274	RAWS	11/1/2004	Present	YES
Barryville 6 NW	41.500	-74.983	183	COOP	11/5/1956	Present	NO
Belvidere	40.833	-75.083	85	COOP	1/1/1893	12/31/1981	NO
Belvidere Bridge	40.829	-75.084	80	COOP	11/1/1967	Present	NO
Belvidere River	40.833	-75.083	70	COOP	9/1/1976	Present	NO

Name	Lat.	Lon.	Elev. (m)	Network	Start	End	In Park?
Blakeslee Corners	41.100	-75.600	503	COOP	5/1/1948	2/1/1983	NO
Bloomingburg 2 SW	41.533	-74.467	396	COOP	11/1/1989	Present	NO
Branchville	41.150	-74.750	177	COOP	8/1/1954	7/1/1982	NO
Canadensis 1 E	41.167	-75.233	393	COOP	10/1/1969	6/30/1970	NO
Canistear Reservoir	41.109	-74.482	335	COOP	8/1/1948	Present	NO
Charlotteburg Reservoir	41.035	-74.423	232	COOP	4/1/1893	Present	NO
Clinton 2 N	40.663	-74.915	107	COOP	11/1/1967	Present	NO
Culvers Lake	41.167	-74.783	232	COOP	4/1/1902	8/31/1954	NO
Dingmans Ferry 3 W	41.217	-74.900	274	COOP	12/9/1982	Present	NO
East Stroudsburg Uni	41.000	-75.167	158	COOP	12/1/1974	9/26/1988	NO
Easton	40.700	-75.200	49	COOP	5/1/1948	12/31/1948	NO
Edgemere	41.267	-75.000	397	COOP	4/1/1949	7/31/1949	NO
Gardnerville	41.346	-74.487	140	COOP	10/1/1956	Present	NO
Gouldsboro	41.250	-75.450	576	COOP	7/1/1914	12/1/1987	NO
Great Meadows 4 N	40.933	-74.917	165	COOP	8/1/1948	3/31/1962	NO
Greentown 4 SE	41.283	-75.250	512	COOP	10/1/1980	Present	NO
Hawley 1 E	41.483	-75.167	271	COOP	11/1/1897	Present	NO
Hawley 1 S	41.467	-75.183	366	COOP	6/1/1934	7/1/1960	NO
Hawley 3 ESE	41.467	-75.133	259	COOP	7/1/1960	Present	NO
Hawley 4 SW	41.450	-75.267	445	COOP	1/1/1928	8/17/1972	NO
High Point Park	41.306	-74.671	463	COOP	11/1/1956	11/1/2005	NO
Hollisterville	41.383	-75.433	418	COOP	1/1/1928	Present	NO
Lake Minisink	41.217	-75.050	415	COOP	5/1/1959	10/1/1987	NO
Long Pond Pocono Lake	41.119	-75.548	549	COOP	1/1/1947	1/1/2001	NO
Long Valley	40.788	-74.779	168	COOP	10/1/1929	11/1/2004	NO
Long Valley 2	40.783	-74.783	165	COOP	5/1/1961	1/16/1963	NO
Macopin Lwr Intk Dam	41.017	-74.400	177	COOP	1/1/1941	Present	NO
Matamoras	41.367	-74.700	128	COOP	10/1/1904	Present	NO
Merwinsburg	40.967	-75.467	300	COOP	7/1/1925	2/1/1996	NO
Middletown 2	41.433	-74.417	153	COOP	6/1/1974	4/30/1980	NO
Middletown 2 NW	41.460	-74.449	213	COOP	1/1/1893	Present	NO
Milanville	41.673	-75.064	232	COOP	8/1/1945	Present	NO
Milton	41.017	-74.533	290	COOP	1/1/1941	3/31/1972	NO
Mongaup Valley 4 SSW	41.617	-74.817	366	COOP	7/25/1945	Present	NO
Mount Pocono 2	41.133	-75.350	570	COOP	10/11/1956	8/31/1969	NO
Narrowsburg 4 SE	41.567	-75.017	226	COOP	11/1/1956	1/1/1999	NO
Newton	41.055	-74.759	184	COOP	1/1/1893	1/1/2006	NO
Oak Ridge Reservoir	41.004	-74.499	268	COOP	1/1/1941	Present	NO
Oakland Valley	41.500	-74.650	280	COOP	5/1/1948	4/1/2004	NO
Paupack 1 WSW	41.400	-75.233	415	COOP	4/1/1926	Present	NO
Pecks Pond	41.283	-75.100	421	COOP	7/29/1945	12/31/1958	NO
Pen Argyl	40.865	-75.246	219	COOP	9/1/1967	Present	NO
Phillipsburg	41.433	-74.367	134	COOP	11/1/1956	9/30/1959	NO
Phillipsburg Easton	40.700	-75.200	61	COOP	1/1/1940	Present	NO
Pickerel Lake	41.250	-75.067	403	COOP	3/1/1959	5/31/1959	NO
Pimple Hill	41.033	-75.500	677	COOP	10/1/1949	11/30/1959	NO

Name	Lat.	Lon.	Elev. (m)	Network	Start	End	In Park?
Port Jervis	41.380	-74.685	143	COOP	5/1/1948	Present	NO
Port Jervis Bridge	41.367	-74.700	0	COOP	1/1/1893	12/31/1948	NO
Portland	40.917	-75.100	92	COOP	5/1/1948	1/31/1956	NO
Pottersville 2 NNW	40.737	-74.732	111	COOP	3/12/1968	Present	NO
Promised Land State	41.300	-75.217	537	COOP	7/1/1971	Present	NO
Prompton Dam	41.589	-75.330	375	COOP	7/1/1958	Present	NO
Rock Hill 3 SW	41.583	-74.617	387	COOP	11/1/1956	Present	NO
Schooleys Mountain	40.800	-74.800	305	COOP	9/1/1960	4/30/1961	NO
South Canaan 1 NE	41.517	-75.400	427	COOP	7/1/1948	5/1/1993	NO
Split Rock Pond	40.967	-74.467	244	COOP	8/1/1948	9/16/1998	NO
Stroudsburg	40.983	-75.183	119	COOP	5/1/1948	11/30/1952	NO
Stroudsburg	41.013	-75.191	140	COOP	12/1/1910	Present	NO
Sussex 2 NE	41.226	-74.571	137	COOP	1/1/1893	Present	NO
Sussex 8 NNW	41.325	-74.645	311	COOP	1/1/1992	11/1/2005	NO
Tannersville 2E	41.054	-75.290	277	COOP	8/1/1925	Present	NO
Tobyhanna Pocono Mtn AP	41.139	-75.223	584	COOP	9/12/1901	Present	NO
Tranquility 2 W	40.950	-74.833	168	COOP	1/1/1956	9/30/1961	NO
Warwick	41.267	-74.367	165	COOP	3/1/1900	12/31/1974	NO
West Wharton	40.900	-74.600	207	COOP	4/1/1959	11/26/1990	NO
Wind Gap 1 S	40.833	-75.300	220	COOP	3/1/1947	9/1/1967	NO
Aeroflex-Andover Arpt.	41.009	-74.737	178	SAO	8/17/1998	Present	NO
Belvidere River	40.833	-75.083	70	SAO	9/1/1976	Present	NO
Mount Pocono	41.139	-75.379	584	SAO	9/29/1999	Present	NO
Sussex Airport	41.200	-74.623	128	SAO	10/25/2000	Present	NO
Tobyhanna Pocono Mtn AP	41.139	-75.223	584	SAO	9/15/1934	Present	NO
Martins Creek	40.783	-75.167	106	WBAN	4/1/1934	4/30/1938	NO
Milford West	41.133	-74.367	229	WBAN	1/1/1946	3/31/1946	NO

Upper Delaware Scenic and Recreational River (UPDE)

Name	Lat.	Lon.	Elev. (m)	Network	Start	End	In Park?
Barryville 6 NW	41.500	-74.983	183	COOP	11/5/1956	Present	YES
Equinunk 2 NW	41.867	-75.267	271	COOP	8/1/1945	Present	YES
Milanville	41.673	-75.064	232	COOP	8/1/1945	Present	YES
Narrowsburg 4 SE	41.567	-75.017	226	COOP	11/1/1956	1/1/1999	YES
Bainbridge 2 E	42.283	-75.450	303	COOP	12/1/1907	1/1/1993	NO
Bainbridge Jennison	42.276	-75.479	296	COOP	3/1/1977	Present	NO
Beerston	42.117	-75.117	473	COOP	12/1/1911	2/28/1951	NO
Bloomingburg 2 SW	41.533	-74.467	396	COOP	11/1/1989	Present	NO
Branchville	41.150	-74.750	177	COOP	8/1/1954	7/1/1982	NO
Butternut Brook	41.917	-74.667	561	COOP	5/1/1948	8/31/1974	NO
Calicon 1 SW	41.750	-75.050	229	COOP	11/1/1979	Present	NO
Callicoon	41.767	-75.050	244	COOP	4/1/1949	6/1/1966	NO
Callicoon 2	41.780	-75.054	396	COOP	5/1/1974	Present	NO
Canadensis 1 E	41.167	-75.233	393	COOP	10/1/1969	6/30/1970	NO
China	42.167	-75.400	445	COOP	9/1/1945	8/1/1968	NO
China 2	42.100	-75.383	351	COOP	2/6/1950	5/14/1970	NO
Cooks Falls	41.950	-74.983	351	COOP	3/1/1976	Present	NO
Craigie Clair	41.967	-74.867	427	COOP	5/1/1948	2/28/1973	NO

Name	Lat.	Lon.	Elev. (m)	Network	Start	End	In Park?
Culvers Lake	41.167	-74.783	232	COOP	4/1/1902	8/31/1954	NO
Deposit	42.063	-75.428	305	COOP	4/1/1953	Present	NO
Dingmans Ferry	41.217	-74.867	131	COOP	11/6/1939	12/8/1982	NO
Dingmans Ferry 3 W	41.217	-74.900	274	COOP	12/9/1982	Present	NO
Downsville	42.083	-75.000	339	COOP	5/1/1948	12/31/1967	NO
Downsville Dam	42.083	-74.967	396	COOP	5/1/1959	Present	NO
East Stroudsburg Univ	41.000	-75.167	158	COOP	12/1/1974	9/26/1988	NO
Edgemere	41.267	-75.000	397	COOP	4/1/1949	7/31/1949	NO
Fishs Eddy	41.967	-75.183	311	COOP	4/1/1953	Present	NO
Gardnerville	41.346	-74.487	140	COOP	10/1/1956	Present	NO
Gouldsboro	41.250	-75.450	576	COOP	7/1/1914	12/1/1987	NO
Greentown 4 SE	41.283	-75.250	512	COOP	10/1/1980	Present	NO
Harpursville	42.150	-75.617	390	COOP	11/1/1944	3/31/1956	NO
Harvard River	42.017	-75.117	307	COOP	1/14/1888	Present	NO
Hawley 1 E	41.483	-75.167	271	COOP	11/1/1897	Present	NO
Hawley 1 S	41.467	-75.183	366	COOP	6/1/1934	7/1/1960	NO
Hawley 3 ESE	41.467	-75.133	259	COOP	7/1/1960	Present	NO
Hawley 4 SW	41.450	-75.267	445	COOP	1/1/1928	8/17/1972	NO
High Point Park	41.306	-74.671	463	COOP	11/1/1956	11/1/2005	NO
Hollisterville	41.383	-75.433	418	COOP	1/1/1928	Present	NO
Honesdale 4 NW	41.617	-75.317	430	COOP	1/1/1944	1/1/1997	NO
Honesdale 5 NNW	41.650	-75.267	317	COOP	1/1/1894	10/8/1980	NO
Jadwyn Dam	41.617	-75.267	335	COOP	10/1/1980	6/26/1985	NO
Lake Minisink	41.217	-75.050	415	COOP	5/1/1959	10/1/1987	NO
Layton 2	41.250	-74.867	122	COOP	4/1/1962	2/12/1973	NO
Layton 3 NW	41.250	-74.850	143	COOP	6/1/1900	2/28/1973	NO
Lewbeach	41.950	-74.833	580	COOP	5/1/1948	8/31/1974	NO
Liberty 1 NE	41.800	-74.733	472	COOP	2/1/1898	Present	NO
Long Pond Pocono Lake	41.119	-75.548	549	COOP	1/1/1947	1/1/2001	NO
Mary Smith	42.050	-74.817	464	COOP	5/1/1948	12/31/1976	NO
Matamoras	41.367	-74.700	128	COOP	10/1/1904	Present	NO
Middletown 2	41.433	-74.417	153	COOP	6/1/1974	4/30/1980	NO
Middletown 2 NW	41.460	-74.449	213	COOP	1/1/1893	Present	NO
Mongaup Valley 4 SSW	41.617	-74.817	366	COOP	7/25/1945	Present	NO
Montague Milford	41.300	-74.800	113	COOP	11/5/1956	6/8/2004	NO
Mount Pocono 2	41.133	-75.350	570	COOP	10/11/1956	8/31/1969	NO
Neversink	41.833	-74.650	397	COOP	5/1/1948	11/30/1974	NO
Newton	41.055	-74.759	184	COOP	1/1/1893	1/1/2006	NO
Oakland Valley	41.500	-74.650	280	COOP	5/1/1948	4/1/2004	NO
Parkston	41.900	-74.817	445	COOP	5/1/1948	8/15/1970	NO
Paupack 1 WSW	41.400	-75.233	415	COOP	4/1/1926	Present	NO
Pecks Pond	41.283	-75.100	421	COOP	7/29/1945	12/31/1958	NO
Phillipsburg	41.433	-74.367	134	COOP	11/1/1956	9/30/1959	NO
Pickerel Lake	41.250	-75.067	403	COOP	3/1/1959	5/31/1959	NO
Pleasant Mount 1 W	41.733	-75.450	548	COOP	10/1/1924	Present	NO
Port Jervis	41.380	-74.685	143	COOP	1/1/1893	Present	NO

Name	Lat.	Lon.	Elev. (m)	Network	Start	End	In Park?
Port Jervis Bridge	41.367	-74.700	0	COOP	5/1/1948	12/31/1948	NO
Promised Land State	41.300	-75.217	537	COOP	7/1/1971	Present	NO
Prompton Dam	41.589	-75.330	375	COOP	7/1/1958	Present	NO
Rock Hill 3 SW	41.583	-74.617	387	COOP	11/1/1956	Present	NO
Roscoe	41.933	-74.900	454	COOP	5/14/1970	Present	NO
South Canaan 1 NE	41.517	-75.400	427	COOP	7/1/1948	5/1/1993	NO
Stillwater Dam	41.683	-75.483	503	COOP	3/1/1960	Present	NO
Stroudsburg	41.013	-75.191	140	COOP	12/1/1910	Present	NO
Susquehanna	41.948	-75.605	277	COOP	2/1/1935	Present	NO
Sussex 2 NE	41.226	-74.571	137	COOP	1/1/1893	Present	NO
Sussex 8 NNW	41.325	-74.645	311	COOP	1/1/1992	11/1/2005	NO
Tannersville 2E	41.054	-75.290	277	COOP	8/1/1925	Present	NO
Terry Clove	42.133	-74.900	421	COOP	5/1/1948	11/30/1974	NO
Tobyhanna Pocono Mtn AP	41.139	-75.223	584	COOP	9/12/1901	Present	NO
Tocks Island	41.017	-75.083	88	COOP	6/1/1967	2/1/1999	NO
Walton	42.167	-75.133	378	COOP	7/1/1956	8/1/1996	NO
Walton 2	42.183	-75.133	451	COOP	8/1/1996	Present	NO
Walton 5 NE	42.233	-75.083	549	COOP	6/1/1900	7/31/1956	NO
Warwick	41.267	-74.367	165	COOP	5/1/1948	12/31/1974	NO
Windsor 2 SE	42.060	-75.614	286	COOP	6/1/1977	Present	NO
Woodbourne	41.750	-74.600	360	COOP	11/1/1979	Present	NO
Loch Lomond	41.204	-74.890	274	RAWS	11/1/2004	Present	NO
Montgomery Orange Co. AP	41.509	-74.265	111	SAO	3/1/1972	Present	NO
Monticello Sullivan	41.700	-74.800	429	SAO	7/1/1969	Present	NO
Mount Pocono	41.139	-75.379	584	SAO	9/29/1999	Present	NO
Sussex Airport	41.200	-74.623	128	SAO	10/25/2000	Present	NO
Tobyhanna Pocono Mtn AP	41.139	-75.223	584	SAO	9/15/1934	Present	NO

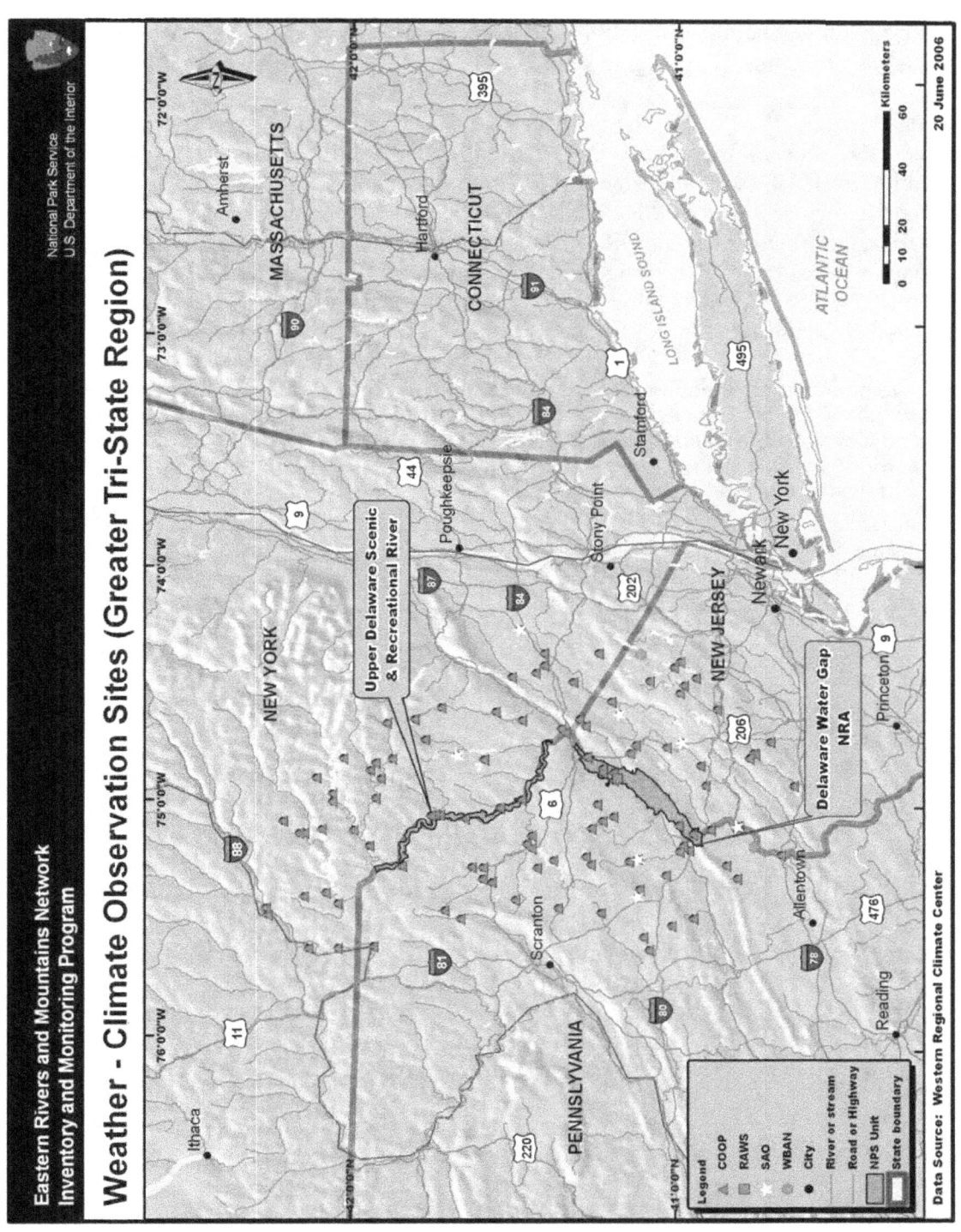

Figure 4.2. Station locations for ERMN park units in the Tri-State region. Some COOP sites are co-labeled as NWS or WBAN.

39

4.2.3. West Virginia Park Units

The only active site within ERMN park units in West Virginia is the Grandview RAWS station in NERI, which has been in operation since 2002 (Table 4.5). In relation to the other two ERMN sub-regions that have been discussed thus far (Pennsylvania, Tri-State area), the West Virginia park units have sparser coverage of weather/climate stations. The stations for ERMN park units in West Virginia are generally 10-20 km apart, whereas elsewhere in ERMN the stations are generally less than 10 km apart (Figure 4.3).

There are no stations listed within the boundaries of BLUE. Currently, there are 14 COOP stations, two RAWS stations, and two SAO stations that are active within 40 km of BLUE. The nearest station to BLUE is the Pipestem RAWS station, which is just south of BLUE (Figure 4.3) and has been in operation since 2004 (Table 4.5). The closest reliable long-term data records are available from the Bluestone Lake COOP, which is only 10 km northeast of BLUE and has data records that go back to 1943. The longest data records are found at the COOP stations "Beckley VA Hospital", "Elkhorn", and "Union 3 SSE". These three stations are all currently active and have operated since the 1890s.

Table 4.5. Weather/climate stations for ERMN park units in West Virginia. Stations inside park units and within 40 km of the park unit boundary are included. Each listing includes station name, location, and elevation; weather/climate network associated with station; operational start/end dates for station; and flag to indicate if station is located inside park unit boundaries. Missing entries are indicated by "M".

Name	Lat.	Lon.	Elev. (m)	Network	Start	End	In Park?
Bluestone River National Scenic River (BLUE)							
Alderson	37.727	-80.659	470	COOP	3/1/1944	Present	NO
Athens	37.423	-81.026	761	COOP	3/23/1940	1/1/2004	NO
Beckley	37.750	-81.250	775	COOP	M	6/30/1964	NO
Beckley Raleigh Co Mem AP	37.784	-81.123	766	COOP	7/1/1952	Present	NO
Beckley VA Hospital	37.765	-81.194	710	COOP	12/1/1893	Present	NO
Bluefield	37.256	-81.226	875	COOP	2/1/1997	Present	NO
Bluefield 2	37.267	-81.217	790	COOP	10/17/1916	1/31/1956	NO
Bluefield 2 NW	37.267	-81.267	796	COOP	10/1/1891	5/31/1967	NO
Bluefield Mercer Co. AP	37.296	-81.208	875	COOP	5/1/1954	Present	NO
Bluefield Mercer Co.	37.283	-81.200	869	COOP	1/1/1956	9/30/1959	NO
Bluestone Lake	37.641	-80.883	424	COOP	3/1/1943	Present	NO
Elkhorn	37.387	-81.405	594	COOP	1/1/1892	Present	NO
Flat Top	37.589	-81.093	1017	COOP	10/1/1930	Present	NO
Glen Lyn	37.373	-80.860	463	COOP	3/1/1914	Present	NO
Hinton 1	37.667	-80.883	436	COOP	1/10/1895	4/30/1949	NO
Hinton 2	37.667	-80.883	415	COOP	8/1/1948	6/30/1949	NO
Lindside	37.480	-80.656	605	COOP	4/5/1940	Present	NO
Matoaka	37.417	-81.250	763	COOP	9/1/1951	10/1/1981	NO
Mullens	37.584	-81.382	430	COOP	2/14/1940	Present	NO
Princeton	37.384	-81.082	723	COOP	6/1/1900	Present	NO
Rhodell	37.600	-81.300	500	COOP	7/1/1974	10/1/1989	NO

Name	Lat.	Lon.	Elev. (m)	Network	Start	End	In Park?
Shady Springs 2 ESE	37.700	-81.050	811	COOP	1/1/1944	6/30/1954	NO
Staffordsville 3 ENE	37.271	-80.713	595	COOP	9/1/1951	Present	NO
Union 3 SSE	37.544	-80.534	643	COOP	2/1/1894	Present	NO
Grandview	37.833	-81.068	918	RAWS	10/1/2002	Present	NO
Pipestem	37.526	-80.999	831	RAWS	12/1/2004	Present	NO
Beckley Raleigh Co Mem AP	37.784	-81.123	766	SAO	7/1/1952	Present	NO
Bluefield Mercer Co. AP	37.296	-81.208	875	SAO	5/1/1954	Present	NO

Gauley River National Recreation Area (GARI)

Name	Lat.	Lon.	Elev. (m)	Network	Start	End	In Park?
Ansted Hawks Nest St. Park	38.121	-81.117	395	COOP	10/1/1999	Present	NO
Belva	38.233	-81.183	244	COOP	9/1/1951	1/31/1982	NO
Birch River	38.502	-80.760	319	COOP	7/1/1965	11/3/1995	NO
Birch River 3 WSW	38.492	-80.802	454	COOP	10/1/1999	7/1/2002	NO
Birch River 4 SW	38.457	-80.793	655	COOP	4/2/2003	10/1/2005	NO
Birch River 6 SSW	38.400	-80.800	576	COOP	10/1/1949	5/16/1967	NO
Camden On Gauley 2 SW	38.357	-80.629	677	COOP	1/7/1915	Present	NO
Clay	38.460	-81.084	223	COOP	4/1/1897	Present	NO
Clay 2	38.467	-81.067	207	COOP	8/1/1948	4/30/1955	NO
Corton	38.486	-81.271	195	COOP	4/1/1955	7/1/1996	NO
Dille 1 NE	38.500	-80.817	390	COOP	2/1/1967	10/1/1987	NO
East Rainelle 3 NNE	38.000	-80.750	738	COOP	1/19/1942	3/1/1981	NO
Hico	38.123	-81.008	713	COOP	12/1/1955	1/1/1998	NO
Hominy Falls	38.133	-80.717	723	COOP	7/1/1965	Present	NO
Jodie	38.233	-81.133	235	COOP	12/1/1960	8/31/1961	NO
Kanawha Falls	38.138	-81.214	189	COOP	6/1/1917	Present	NO
London Locks	38.195	-81.371	189	COOP	7/1/1934	Present	NO
London Locks Upper	38.200	-81.367	189	COOP	8/1/1948	12/31/1948	NO
Lookout	38.067	-80.967	610	COOP	9/1/1951	1/31/1952	NO
Lookout 2	38.067	-80.967	702	COOP	12/1/1952	12/31/1955	NO
McRoss	37.983	-80.750	746	COOP	9/1/1955	4/1/1988	NO
McRoss 3 E	37.990	-80.680	976	COOP	4/1/1988	Present	NO
Mount Nebo 1 S	38.189	-80.849	595	COOP	4/1/1994	Present	NO
Oak Hill	37.971	-81.151	622	COOP	10/10/1941	Present	NO
Queen Shoals	38.471	-81.284	189	COOP	12/1/1952	Present	NO
Rainelle	37.967	-80.783	738	COOP	9/18/1930	7/31/1955	NO
Richwood	38.233	-80.533	746	COOP	1/12/1961	2/1/1985	NO
Richwood	38.233	-80.550	732	COOP	9/1/1951	7/27/1978	NO
Richwood	38.250	-80.550	668	COOP	8/1/1948	5/31/1951	NO
Richwood 3 NNE	38.260	-80.517	930	COOP	8/1/1930	8/14/1960	NO
Sanderson	38.367	-81.367	220	COOP	8/27/1960	1/1/1990	NO
Summersville	38.283	-80.833	589	COOP	1/17/1901	7/25/1966	NO
Summersville Lake	38.221	-80.894	537	COOP	7/1/1966	Present	NO
Thurmond	37.950	-81.083	326	COOP	5/1/1985	7/1/1991	NO
Widen	38.467	-80.867	348	COOP	8/1/1960	2/15/1967	NO
Grandview	37.833	-81.068	918	RAWS	10/1/2002	Present	NO

New River Gorge National River (NERI)

Name	Lat.	Lon.	Elev. (m)	Network	Start	End	In Park?
Thurmond	37.950	-81.083	326	COOP	5/1/1985	7/1/1991	YES
Grandview	37.833	-81.068	918	RAWS	10/1/2002	Present	YES
Alderson	37.727	-80.659	470	COOP	3/1/1944	Present	NO
Ansted Hawks Nest St. Park	38.121	-81.117	395	COOP	10/1/1999	Present	NO
Athens	37.423	-81.026	761	COOP	3/23/1940	1/1/2004	NO
Beckley	37.750	-81.250	775	COOP	M	6/30/1964	NO
Beckley Raleigh Co Mem AP	37.784	-81.123	766	COOP	7/1/1952	Present	NO
Beckley VA Hospital	37.765	-81.194	710	COOP	12/1/1893	Present	NO
Belva	38.233	-81.183	244	COOP	9/1/1951	1/31/1982	NO
Bluestone Lake	37.641	-80.883	424	COOP	3/1/1943	Present	NO
Dry Creek	37.859	-81.465	385	COOP	12/1/1961	Present	NO
East Rainelle 3 NNE	38.000	-80.750	738	COOP	1/19/1942	3/1/1981	NO
Flat Top	37.589	-81.093	1017	COOP	10/1/1930	Present	NO
Hico	38.123	-81.008	713	COOP	12/1/1955	1/1/1998	NO
Hinton 1	37.667	-80.883	436	COOP	1/10/1895	4/30/1949	NO
Hinton 2	37.667	-80.883	415	COOP	8/1/1948	6/30/1949	NO
Hominy Falls	38.133	-80.717	723	COOP	7/1/1965	Present	NO
Jodie	38.233	-81.133	235	COOP	12/1/1960	8/31/1961	NO
Kanawha Falls	38.138	-81.214	189	COOP	6/1/1917	Present	NO
Kayford	38.017	-81.450	409	COOP	10/1/1916	12/31/1952	NO
Lewisburg 3 N	37.856	-80.403	702	COOP	9/11/1852	Present	NO
London Locks	38.195	-81.371	189	COOP	7/1/1934	Present	NO
London Locks Upper	38.200	-81.367	189	COOP	8/1/1948	12/31/1948	NO
Lookout	38.067	-80.967	610	COOP	9/1/1951	1/31/1952	NO
Lookout 2	38.067	-80.967	702	COOP	12/1/1952	12/31/1955	NO
McRoss	37.983	-80.750	746	COOP	9/1/1955	4/1/1988	NO
McRoss 3 E	37.990	-80.680	976	COOP	4/1/1988	Present	NO
Mount Nebo 1 S	38.189	-80.849	595	COOP	4/1/1994	Present	NO
Mullens	37.584	-81.382	430	COOP	2/14/1940	Present	NO
Naoma	37.867	-81.483	369	COOP	12/16/1940	2/13/1980	NO
Oak Hill	37.971	-81.151	622	COOP	10/10/1941	Present	NO
Rainelle	37.967	-80.783	738	COOP	9/18/1930	7/31/1955	NO
Ravencliff 1 N	37.700	-81.483	549	COOP	6/1/1974	8/1/1986	NO
Rhodell	37.600	-81.300	500	COOP	7/1/1974	10/1/1989	NO
Shady Springs 2 ESE	37.700	-81.050	811	COOP	1/1/1944	6/30/1954	NO
Smoot	37.883	-80.667	747	COOP	6/1/1961	4/7/1964	NO
Summersville	38.283	-80.833	589	COOP	1/17/1901	7/25/1966	NO
Summersville Lake	38.221	-80.894	537	COOP	7/1/1966	Present	NO
Whitesville	37.988	-81.543	251	COOP	10/1/2001	Present	NO
Pipestem	37.526	-80.999	831	RAWS	12/1/2004	Present	NO
Beckley Raleigh Co Mem AP	37.784	-81.123	766	SAO	7/1/1952	Present	NO

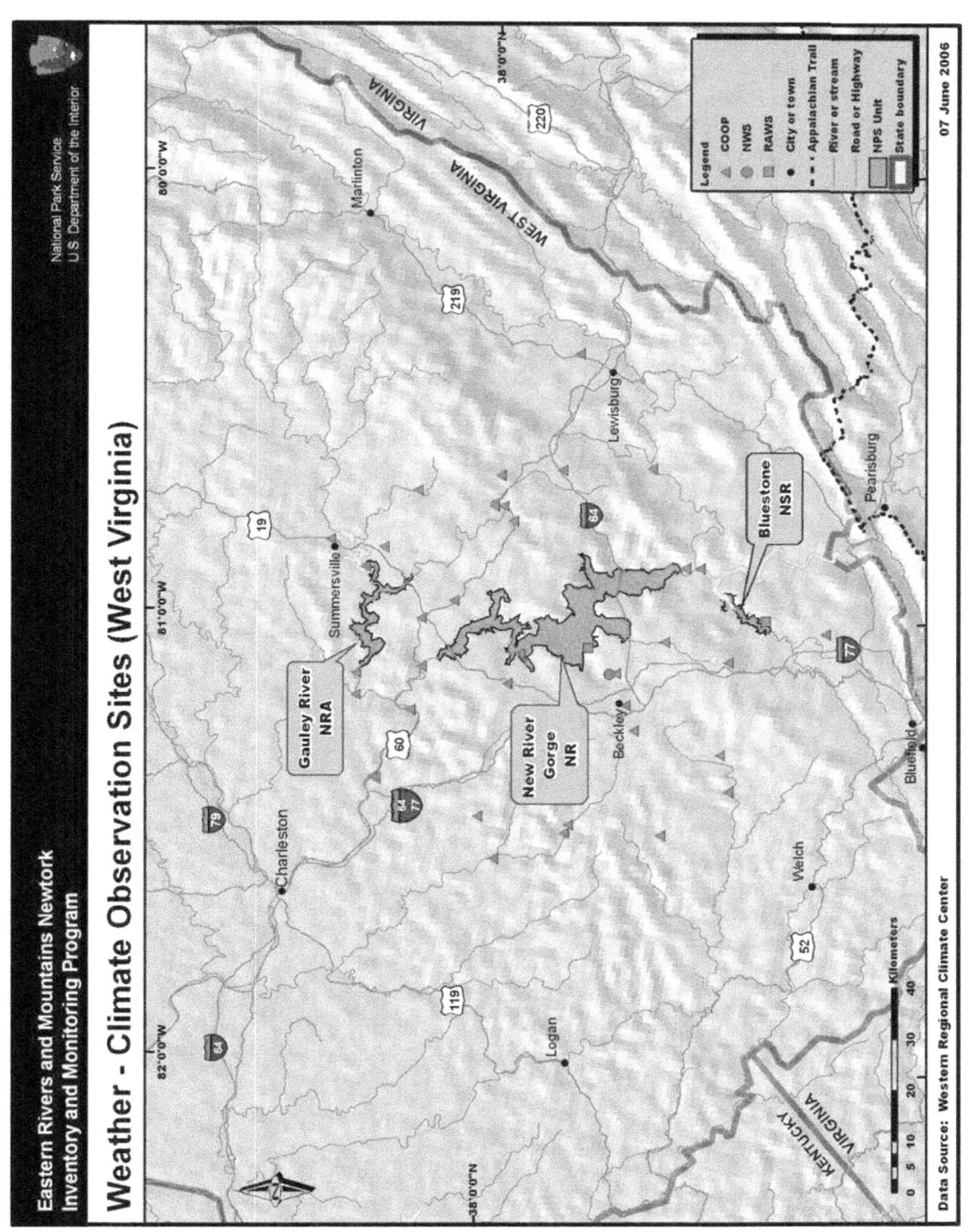

Figure 4.3. Station locations for ERMN park units in West Virginia. The SAO sites are co-labeled as NWS.

43

Like BLUE, there are no stations listed within the boundaries of GARI. Currently, there are 11 active COOP stations and one active RAWS station within 40 km of GARI. The nearest station to GARI is the COOP station "Summersville Lake." This station is located at Summersville Lake just outside the east boundary of GARI. It has been active since 1966 and has a largely complete data record. The nearest station to GARI that provides near-real-time observations is the Grandview RAWS station (Table 4.5), which is almost 40 km south of GARI, inside the boundaries of NERI (Figure 4.3). There are two COOP sites (Belva and Jodie) that were located between 5-10 km west of the westernmost boundary of GARI, but these stations are no longer active. The longest data records for the stations within 40 km of GARI are available from several COOP stations whose data go back as far as the 1890s. Oak Hill and London Locks (Table 4.5) has reliable data records of both temperature and precipitation that go back to the 1930s and 1940s and are almost complete with the exception of occasional gaps lasting up to a few months in duration. The COOP station "Camden on Gauley 2 SW" only measures precipitation, while Clay was a precipitation-only COOP station until the early 1990s.

As previously mentioned, NERI has the only active weather/climate station located within any ERMN park unit in West Virginia. This site is the Grandview RAWS station, which provides near-real-time observations and has been active since 2002. There was a COOP station (Thurmond) that was active in NERI from 1985 to 1991 and was located in the northern portion of NERI. Since the Grandview RAWS station is centrally located in NERI, both the northern and southern portions of NERI are not currently sampled by any weather/climate stations. Stations within 40 km of NERI that are currently active include 17 COOP stations, one RAWS station (Pipestem), and one SAO station (Beckley Raleigh Co. Mem. AP; see Table 4.5). There are a few COOP stations in the NERI vicinity that have data records extending back to the 1800s (Table 4.5). Of these sites, the longest records are available from the COOP site "Lewisburg 3 N".

5.0. Conclusions and Recommendations

We have based our findings on an examination of the available records and the environmental characteristics of ERMN park units, discussions with NPS staff and other collaborators, and prior knowledge of the area. Here, we offer an evaluation and general comments pertaining to the status, prospects, and needs for climate-monitoring capabilities in ERMN. Much preliminary work has been accomplished by the Pennsylvania State Climate Office to identify weather/climate stations within ERMN park units, particularly those in Pennsylvania. This report builds on these previous station inventories and suggestions for investigative climate protocols.

5.1. Eastern Rivers and Mountains Inventory and Monitoring Network

Most of the park units in ERMN had no stations at or within park boundaries. This is not surprising, due to the relatively small sizes of the ERMN park units. Four (out of nine) of the ERMN park units are historical sites such as battlefields or other memorials. Sites such as these are quite small and therefore must rely heavily on stations outside of the park units for their weather and climate data. This is particularly common in the ERMN park units in Pennsylvania. Fortunately, there are numerous manual and automated weather/climate stations around the ERMN park units in Pennsylvania.

Despite this, the decrease in climate stations at JOFL in recent years is unfortunate, given the emphasis of this park unit on a significant historical storm event (the Johnstown flood of 1889), and subsequent flood events in the region such as those in 1977. It would be beneficial for NPS to make every effort to encourage the continuation of any climate stations that are currently active near JOFL, particularly those stations with longer data records. The active use of data from such stations for JOFL visitor education activities could be very beneficial by actively illustrating characteristics of climate extremes, an important theme upon which this park unit is based. These efforts could include partnering with an automated weather station network, such as the RAWS program, to encourage the installation of a real-time station at JOFL.

Long data records could potentially be available for FRHI from those COOP stations around Grays Landing. Although they are indicated by our station lists to be distinct stations, the identical locations suggest that these could actually be one site that has merely had changes in station name, observers, etc. The combined data records go back to the late 1940s and could be used in some instances for climate analyses in the local area. However, because of the existing uncertainties about station identities, we would caution against the widespread use of these data for such climate analyses.

Park units in the Tri-State region of ERMN also have numerous nearby weather/climate stations. However, there are existing gaps in station coverage that could be addressed. The installation of a manual COOP station in the south-central portions of DEWA could be beneficial for documenting local-scale precipitation patterns in the park unit, particularly during spring and summer months when convective precipitation patterns with high spatial variability are common. The RAWS site currently operating in DEWA should provide satisfactory real-time weather data for the park unit, along with the nearby SAO sites. To the north, however, the closest real-time observations to UPDE are available from a SAO station that is 20 km east of the park unit.

45

Therefore, it may be advantageous to have an automated station installed somewhere within UPDE. Since the RAWS network already has a presence in the area (e.g. the RAWS station in DEWA), we would recommend that NPS consider working with the RAWS program to encourage the installation of a RAWS station at UPDE. Stratification of weather/climate station coverage by watershed or by elevation and elevation gradients (beyond the scope of this project) may reveal additional coverage gaps that need to be addressed.

The existing RAWS sites in and near BLUE and NERI provide near-real-time weather data for the watershed that includes the New River and Bluestone River. Despite the general scarcity of weather and climate stations in these two park units, the two RAWS stations do provide near-real-time weather observations for the watershed, which can be very valuable particularly during passages of tropical storms or other convective precipitation events that can result in significant flooding. It is not clear, on the other hand, if there are similar stations that are currently active in the Gauley River watershed. At a minimum, it is important that NPS work with NWS to ensure that the existing manual COOP site at Summersville Lake is retained for the purpose of long-term climate monitoring near GARI. However, this site could be enhanced by adding an automated RAWS site such as those in and near BLUE and NERI. Access to near-real-time weather conditions near GARI would be useful both for managing recreational activities and for monitoring ecosystem characteristics along the Gauley River.

5.2. Spatial Variations in Mean Climate

When installing new stations, the primary goal should be overall characterization of the main climate elements (temperature and precipitation). This level of characterization generally requires that (a) stations should not be located in deep valley bottoms (cold air drainage pockets) or near excessively steep slopes and (b) stations should be distributed spatially in the major biomes of each park. If there is already dense station coverage in a given area, additional stations would be best used for two important and somewhat competing purposes: (a) add redundancy as backup for loss of data from current stations (or loss of the physical stations) or (b) provide added information on spatial heterogeneity in climate arising from topographic diversity.

5.3. Climate Change Detection

The desire for credible, accurate, complete, and long-term climate records—from any location—cannot be overemphasized. Thus, this consideration always should have a high priority. Consistency in these data records is also important in the ERMN. Compared to other regions in the U.S., the magnitudes of the observed temperature and precipitation trends in the ERMN are relatively small, making the trends harder to detect amid any existing discontinuities in the data record due to artificial changes such as station moves or changes in instrumentation. Long-term rural stations are particularly valuable in this regard. Because of spatial diversity in climate, monitoring efforts that fill knowledge gaps and provide information on long-term temporal variability in short-distance relationships also will be valuable. We cannot be sure that climate variability and climate change will affect all parts of the ERMN equally. In fact, it is appropriate to speculate that this is not the case, and spatial variations in temporal variability extend to small spatial scales (a few kilometers or less in some cases).

5.4. Aesthetics

This issue arises frequently enough to deserve comment. Standards for quality climate measurements require open exposures away from heat sources, buildings, pavement, close vegetation and tall trees, and human intrusion (thus away from property lines). By their nature, sites that meet these standards are usually quite visible. In many settings (such as heavily forested areas) these sites also are quite rare, making them precisely the same places that managers wish to protect from aesthetic intrusion. The most suitable and scientifically defensible sites frequently are rejected as candidate locations for weather/climate stations. Most weather/climate stations, therefore, tend to be "hidden" but many of these hidden locations have inferior exposures. Some measure of compromise is nearly always called for in siting weather and climate stations.

The public has vast interest and curiosity in weather and climate, and within the NPS I&M networks, such measurements consistently rate near or at the top of desired public information. There seem to be many possible opportunities for exploiting and embracing this widespread interest within the interpretive mission of the NPS. One way to do this would be to highlight rather than hide these stations and educate the public about the need for adequate siting. A number of weather displays we have encountered during visits have proven inadvertently to serve as counterexamples for how measurements should not be made.

5.5. Information Access

Access to information promotes its use, which in turn promotes attention to station care and maintenance, better data, and more use. An end-to-end view that extends from sensing to decision support is far preferable to isolated and disconnected activities and aids the support infrastructure that is ultimately so necessary for successful, long-term climate monitoring.

Decisions about improvements in monitoring capacity are facilitated greatly by the ability to examine available climate information. Various methods are being created at WRCC to improve access to that information. Web pages providing historic and ongoing climate data, and information from ERMN park units can be accessed at http://www.wrcc.dri.edu/nps. In the event that this URL changes, there still will be links from the main WRCC Web page entitled "Projects" under NPS.

The WRCC has been steadily developing software to summarize data from hourly sites. This has been occurring under the aegis of the RAWS program and a growing array of product generators ranging from daily and monthly data lists to wind roses and hourly frequency distributions. All park data are available to park personnel via an access code (needed only for data listings) that can be acquired by request. The WRCC RAWS Web page is located at http://www.wrcc.dri.edu/wraws or http://www.raws.dri.edu.

Web pages have been developed to provide access not only to historic and ongoing climate data and information from ERMN park units but also to climate-monitoring efforts for ERMN. These pages can be found through http://www.wrcc.dri.edu/nps.

Additional access to more standard climate information is accessible though the previously mentioned Web pages, as well as through http://www.wrcc.dri.edu/summary. These summaries are generally for COOP stations.

5.6. Summarized Conclusions and Recommendations

- Much work already has been done by ERMN to locate weather/climate stations. This has been accomplished through partnerships with the Pennsylvania State Climate Office.
- Near-real-time precipitation observations are valuable, particularly for monitoring potential flooding events such as those caused by tropical storms and convective events during the spring and summer.
- Park units in West Virginia have the sparsest coverage of weather/climate stations in ERMN. Strategic installation of real-time site (e.g. RAWS) near GARI could be beneficial.
- Climate history is a major theme of JOFL and is a large component of visitor education programs for JOFL. It is therefore important to actively retain existing stations near JOFL that preserve the region's climate history and to take advantage of any opportunities to install a real-time station in or near JOFL.

6.0. Literature Cited

American Association of State Climatologists. 1985. Heights and exposure standards for sensors on automated weather stations. The State Climatologist **9**.

Ayres M. P., and M. J. Lombadero. 2000. Assessing the consequences of global change for forest disturbances from herbivores and pathogens. The Science of the Total Environment **262**:263-286.

Bonan, G. B. 2002. Ecological Climatology: Concepts and Applications. Cambridge University Press.

Bureau of Land Management. 1997. Remote Automatic Weather Station (RAWS) and Remote Environmental Monitoring Systems (REMS) standards. RAWS/REMS Support Facility, Boise, Idaho.

Chapin III, F. S., M. S. Torn, and M. Tateno. 1996. Principles of ecosystem sustainability. The American Naturalist **148**:1016-1037.

Daly, C., R. P. Neilson, and D. L. Phillips. 1994. A statistical-topographic model for mapping climatological precipitation over mountainous terrain. Journal of Applied Meteorology **33**:140-158.

Daly, C., W. P. Gibson, G. H. Taylor, G. L. Johnson, and P. Pasteris. 2002. A knowledge-based approach to the statistical mapping of climate. Climate Research **22**:99-113.

Doggett, M., C. Daly, J. Smith, W. Gibson, G. Taylor, G. Johnson, and P. Pasteris. 2004. High-resolution 1971-2000 mean monthly temperature maps for the western United States. Fourteenth AMS Conf. on Applied Climatology, 84th AMS Annual Meeting. Seattle, WA, American Meteorological Society, Boston, MA, January 2004, Paper 4.3, CD-ROM.

Environmental Protection Agency. 1987. On-site meteorological program guidance for regulatory modeling applications. EPA-450/4-87-013. Environmental Protection Agency, Office of Air Quality Planning and Standards, Research Triangle Park, NC.

Finklin, A. I., and W. C. Fischer. 1990. Weather station handbook –an interagency guide for wildland managers. NFES No. 2140. National Wildfire Coordinating Group, Boise, Idaho.

Fisher, A., et al., 2000. Mid-Atlantic overview. Online. (http://www.essc.psu.edu/mara/results/foundations_report/index.html#report.) Accessed 6 May 2006.

Gibson, W. P., C. Daly, T. Kittel, D. Nychka, C. Johns, N. Rosenbloom, A. McNab, and G. Taylor. 2002. Development of a 103-year high-resolution climate data set for the conterminous United States. Thirteenth AMS Conf. on Applied Climatology. Portland, OR, American Meteorological Society, Boston, MA, May 2002:181-183.

Groisman P. Ya., R. W. Knight, and T. R. Karl. 2000. Heavy precipitation and high streamflow in the contiguous United States: trends in the 20th Century. Bull. Amer. Meteor. Soc. **82**:219-246.

Hughes P. Y., E. H. Mason, T. R. Karl, and W. A. Brower. 1992. United States Historical Climatology Network daily temperature and precipitation data. Environmental Sciences Division Publication 3778, Carbon Dioxide Information and Analysis Center, Oak Ridge National Laboratory, Oak Ridge, Tennessee.

I&M. 2006. I&M Inventories home page. http://science.nature.nps.gov/im/inventory/index.cfm.

Irland, L. C. 2000. Ice storms and forest impacts. The Science of the Total Environment **262**:231-242.

Iverson, L. R., A. M. Prasad, B. J. Hale, and E. K. Sutherland. 1999. An atlas of current and potential future distributions of common trees of the eastern United States, General Technical Report, USDA Forest Service, Northeastern Forest Experiment Station, Radnor, Pennsylvania.

Iverson, L. R., and A. M. Prasad. 2001. Potential changes in tree species richness and forest community types following climate change. Ecosystems **4**:186-199.

Jacobson, M. C., R. J. Charlson, H. Rodhe, and G. H. Orians. 2000. Earth System Science: From Biogeochemical Cycles to Global Change. Academic Press, San Diego.

Karl, T. R., P. Ya. Groisman, R. W. Knight, and R. R. Heim, Jr. 1993. Recent variations of snow cover and snowfall in North America and their relation to precipitation and temperature variations. Journal of Climate **6**:1327-1344.

Karl, T. R., V. E. Derr, D. R. Easterling, C. K. Folland, D. J. Hoffman, S. Levitus, N. Nicholls, D. E. Parker, and G. W. Withee. 1996a. Critical issues for long-term climate monitoring. Pages 55-92 *in* T. R. Karl, editor. Long Term Climate Monitoring by the Global Climate Observing System, Kluwer Publishing.

Karl, T. R., R. W. Knight, D. R. Easterling, and R. G. Quayle, 1996b. Trends in U.S. climate during the twentieth century. Consequences **1**:2-12.

Karl, T. R., and R. W. Knight. 1998. Secular trends in precipitation amount, frequency, and intensity in the United States. Bull. Amer. Meteor. Soc. **79**:231-241.

Lugo, A. E. 2000. Effects and outcomes of hurricanes in a climate change scenario. The Science of the Total Environment **262**:243-252.

Lugo, A. E., and F. N. Scatena. 1996. Background and catastrophic tree mortality in tropical moist, wet, and rain forests. Biotropica **28**:585-599.

Lyons, S. W. 2004. U.S. tropical cyclone landfall variability: 1950-2002. Weather and Forecasting **19**:473-480.

Mahan, C. G. 2004. A natural resource assessment for New River Gorge National River. Natural Resource Report NPA/NERCHAL/NRR-04/006. U.S. Department of Interior, National Park Service, Northeast Region, Philadelphia, PA.

Marshall, M., and N. Piekielek, 2005. Eastern Rivers and Mountains Inventory and Monitoring Network, Vital Signs Monitoring Program, Phase II Report. National Park Service, Eastern Rivers and Mountains Network, National Park Service Inventory and Monitoring Program, University Park, Pennsylvania.

National Assessment Synthesis Team. 2001. Climate Change Impacts on the United States: The Potential Consequences of Climate Variability and Change, Report for the U.S. Global Change Research Program. Cambridge University Press, Cambridge, UK.

National Research Council. 2001. A Climate Services Vision: First Steps Toward the Future. National Academies Press, Washington, D.C.

National Wildfire Coordinating Group. 2004. National fire danger rating system weather station standards. Report PMS 426.3. National Wildfire Coordinating Group, Boise, Idaho.

Neilson, R. P. 1987. Biotic regionalization and climatic controls in western North America. Vegetatio **70**:135-147.

Oakley, K. L., L. P. Thomas, and S. G. Fancy. 2003. Guidelines for long-term monitoring protocols. Wildlife Society Bulletin **31**:1000-1003.

Schlesinger, W. H. 1997. Biogeochemistry: An Analysis of Global Change. Academic Press, San Diego.

Shaver, G. R., J. Canadell, F. S. Chapin III, J. Gurevitch, J. Harte, G. Henry, P. Ineson, S. Jonasson, J. Melillo, L. Pitelka, and others. 2000. Global warming and terrestrial ecosystems: a conceptual framework for analysis. BioScience **50**:871-882.

Smith, E. 1999. Atlantic and East Coast hurricanes 1900-98: a frequency and intensity study for the twenty-first century. Bull. Amer. Meteor. Soc. **80**:2717-2720.

Tanner, B. D. 1990. Automated weather stations. Remote Sensing Reviews **5**:73-98.

World Meteorological Organization. 1983. Guide to meteorological instruments and methods of observation, No. 8, 5th edition, World Meteorological Organization, Geneva Switzerland.

World Meteorological Organization. 2005. Organization and planning of intercomparisons of rainfall intensity gauges. World Meteorological Organization, Geneva Switzerland.

Appendix A. Climate-monitoring principles.

Since the late 1990s, frequent references have been made to a set of climate-monitoring principles enunciated in 1996 by Tom Karl, director of the NOAA NCDC in Asheville, North Carolina. These monitoring principles also have been referred to informally as the "Ten Commandments of Climate Monitoring." Both versions are given here. In addition, these principles have been adopted by the Global Climate Observing System (GCOS 2004).

(Compiled by Kelly Redmond, Western Regional Climate Center, Desert Research Institute, August 2000.)

A.1. Full Version (Karl et al. 1996)

A. Effects on climate records of instrument changes, observing practices, observation locations, sampling rates, etc., must be known before such changes are implemented. This can be ascertained through a period where overlapping measurements from old and new observing systems are collected or sometimes by comparing the old and new observing systems with a reference standard. Site stability for in situ measurements, both in terms of physical location and changes in the nearby environment, also should be a key criterion in site selection. Thus, many synoptic network stations, which are primarily used in weather forecasting but also provide valuable climate data, and dedicated climate stations intended to be operational for extended periods must be subject to this policy.

B. Processing algorithms and changes in these algorithms must be well documented. Documentation should be carried with the data throughout the data-archiving process.

C. Knowledge of instrument, station, and/or platform history is essential for interpreting and using the data. Changes in instrument sampling time, local environmental conditions for in situ measurements, and other factors pertinent to interpreting the observations and measurements should be recorded as a mandatory part in the observing routine and be archived with the original data.

D. In situ and other observations with a long, uninterrupted record should be maintained. Every effort should be applied to protect the data sets that have provided long-term, homogeneous observations. "Long-term" for space-based measurements is measured in decades, but for more conventional measurements, "long-term" may be a century or more. Each element in the observational system should develop a list of prioritized sites or observations based on their contribution to long-term climate monitoring.

E. Calibration, validation, and maintenance facilities are critical requirements for long-term climatic data sets. Homogeneity in the climate record must be assessed routinely, and corrective action must become part of the archived record.

F. Where feasible, some level of "low-technology" backup to "high-technology" observing systems should be developed to safeguard against unexpected operational failures.

G. Regions having insufficient data, variables and regions sensitive to change, and key measurements lacking adequate spatial and temporal resolution should be given the highest priority in designing and implementing new climate-observing systems.

H. Network designers and instrument engineers must receive long-term climate requirements at the outset of the network design process. This is particularly important because most observing systems have been designed for purposes other than long-term climate monitoring. Instruments must possess adequate accuracy with biases small enough to document climate variations and changes.

I. Much of the development of new observational capabilities and the evidence supporting the value of these observations stem from research-oriented needs or programs. A lack of stable, long-term commitment to these observations and lack of a clear transition plan from research to operations are two frequent limitations in the development of adequate, long-term monitoring capabilities. Difficulties in securing a long-term commitment must be overcome in order to improve the climate-observing system in a timely manner with minimal interruptions.

J. Data management systems that facilitate access, use, and interpretation are essential. Freedom of access, low cost, mechanisms that facilitate use (directories, catalogs, browse capabilities, availability of metadata on station histories, algorithm accessibility and documentation, etc.) and quality control should guide data management. International cooperation is critical for successful management of data used to monitor long-term climate change and variability.

A.2. Abbreviated version, "Ten Commandments of Climate Monitoring"

A. Assess the impact of new climate-observing systems or changes to existing systems before they are implemented.

"Thou shalt properly manage network change." (assess effects of proposed changes)

B. Require a suitable period where measurement from new and old climate-observing systems will overlap.

"Thou shalt conduct parallel testing." (compare old and replacement systems)

C. Treat calibration, validation, algorithm-change, and data-homogeneity assessments with the same care as the data.

"Thou shalt collect metadata." (fully document system and operating procedures)

D. Verify capability for routinely assessing the quality and homogeneity of the data including high-resolution data for extreme events.

"Thou shalt assure data quality and continuity." (assess as part of routine operating procedures)

E. Integrate assessments like those conducted by the International Panel on Climate Change into global climate-observing priorities.

"Thou shalt anticipate the use of data." (integrated environmental assessment; component in operational plan for system)

F. Maintain long-term weather and climate stations.

"Thou shalt worship historic significance." (maintain homogeneous data sets from long–term, climate-observing systems)

G. Place high priority on increasing observations in regions lacking sufficient data and in regions sensitive to change and variability.

"Thou shalt acquire complementary data." (new sites to fill observational gaps)

H. Provide network operators, designers, and instrument engineers with long-term requirements at the outset of the design and implementation phases for new systems.

"Thou shalt specify requirements for climate observation systems." (application and usage of observational data)

I. Carefully consider the transition from research-observing system to long-term operation.

"Thou shalt have continuity of purpose." (stable long-term commitments)

J. Focus on data-management systems that facilitate access, use, and interpretation of weather data and metadata.

"Thou shalt provide access to data and metadata." (readily-available weather and climate information)

A.3. Literature Cited

Karl, T. R., V. E. Derr, D. R. Easterling, C. K. Folland, D. J. Hoffman, S. Levitus, N. Nicholls, D. E. Parker, and G. W. Withee. 1996. Critical issues for long-term climate monitoring. Pages 55-92 *in* T. R. Karl, editor. Long Term Climate Monitoring by the Global Climate Observing System, Kluwer Publishing.

Global Climate Observing System. 2004. Implementation plan for the global observing system for climate in support of the UNFCCC. GCOS-92, WMO/TD No. 1219, World Meteorological Organization, Geneva, Switzerland.

Appendix B. Glossary.

Climate—Complete and entire ensemble of statistical descriptors of temporal and spatial properties comprising the behavior of the atmosphere. These descriptors include means, variances, frequency distributions, autocorrelations, spatial correlations and other patterns of association, temporal lags, and element-to-element relationships. The descriptors have a physical basis in flows and reservoirs of energy and mass. Climate and weather phenomena shade gradually into each other and are ultimately inseparable.

Climate Element—(same as Weather Element) Attribute or property of the state of the atmosphere that is measured, estimated, or derived. Examples of climate elements include temperature, wind speed, wind direction, precipitation amount, precipitation type, relative humidity, dewpoint, solar radiation, snow depth, soil temperature at a given depth, etc. A derived element is a function of other elements (like degree days or number of days with rain) and is not measured directly with a sensor. The terms "parameter" or "variable" are not used to describe elements.

Climate Network—Group of climate stations having a common purpose; the group is often owned and maintained by a single organization.

Climate Station—Station where data are collected to track atmospheric conditions over the long-term. Often, this station operates to additional standards to verify long-term consistency. For these stations, the detailed circumstances surrounding a set of measurements (siting and exposure, instrument changes, etc.) are important.

Data—Measurements specifying the state of the physical environment. Does not include metadata.

Data Inventory—Information about overall data properties for each station within a weather or climate network. A data inventory may include start/stop dates, percentages of available data, breakdowns by climate element, counts of actual data values, counts or fractions of data types, etc. These properties must be determined by actually reading the data and thus require the data to be available, accessible, and in a readable format.

NPS I&M Network—A set of NPS park units grouped by a common theme, typically by natural resource and/or geographic region.

Metadata—Information necessary to interpret environmental data properly, organized as a history or series of snapshots—data about data. Examples include details of measurement processes, station circumstances and exposures, assumptions about the site, network purpose and background, types of observations and sensors, pre-treatment of data, access information, maintenance history and protocols, observational methods, archive locations, owner, and station start/end period.

Quality Assurance—Planned and systematic set of activities to provide adequate confidence that products and services are resulting in credible and correct information. Includes quality control.

Quality Control—Evaluation, assessment, and improvement of imperfect data by utilizing other imperfect data.

Station Inventory—Information about a set of stations obtained from metadata that accompany the network or networks. A station inventory can be compiled from direct and indirect reports prepared by others.

Weather—Instantaneous state of the atmosphere at any given time, mainly with respect to its effects on biological activities. As distinguished from climate, weather consists of the short-term (minutes to days) variations in the atmosphere. Popularly, weather is thought of in terms of temperature, precipitation, humidity, wind, sky condition, visibility, and cloud conditions.

Weather Element (same as Climate Element)—Attribute or property of the state of the atmosphere that is measured, estimated, or derived. Examples of weather elements include temperature, wind speed, wind direction, precipitation amount, precipitation type, relative humidity, dewpoint, solar radiation, snow depth, soil temperature at a given depth, etc. A derived weather element is a function of other elements (like degree days or number of days with rain) and is not measured directly. The terms "parameter" and "variable" are not used to describe weather elements.

Weather Network—Group of weather stations usually owned and maintained by a particular organization and usually for a specific purpose.

Weather Station—Station where collected data are intended for near-real-time use with less need for reference to long-term conditions. In many cases, the detailed circumstances of a set of measurements (siting and exposure, instrument changes, etc.) from weather stations are not as important as for climate stations.

Appendix C. Factors in operating a climate network.

C.1. Climate versus Weather
- Climate measurements require _consistency through time._

C.2. Network Purpose
- Anticipated or desired lifetime.
- Breadth of network mission (commitment by needed constituency).
- Dedicated constituency—no network survives without a dedicated constituency.

C.3. Site Identification and Selection
- Spanning gradients in climate or biomes with transects.
- Issues regarding representative spatial scale—site uniformity versus site clustering.
- Alignment with and contribution to network mission.
- Exposure—ability to measure representative quantities.
- Logistics—ability to service station (Always or only in favorable weather?).
- Site redundancy (positive for quality control, negative for extra resources).
- Power—is AC needed?
- Site security—is protection from vandalism needed?
- Permitting often a major impediment and usually underestimated.

C.4. Station Hardware
- Survival—weather is the main cause of lost weather/climate data.
- Robustness of sensors—ability to measure and record in any condition.
- Quality—distrusted records are worthless and a waste of time and money.
  - High quality—will cost up front but pays off later.
  - Low quality—may provide a lower start-up cost but will cost more later (low cost can be expensive).
- Redundancy—backup if sensors malfunction.
- Ice and snow—measurements are much more difficult than rain measurements.
- Severe environments (expense is about two–three times greater than for stations in more benign settings).

C.5. Communications
- Reliability—live data have a much larger constituency.
- One-way or two-way.
  - Retrieval of missed transmissions.
  - Ability to reprogram data logger remotely.
  - Remote troubleshooting abilities.
  - Continuing versus one-time costs.
- Back-up procedures to prevent data loss during communication outages.
- Live communications increase problems but also increase value.

C.6. Maintenance
- Main reason why networks fail (and most networks do eventually fail!).

- <u>Key</u> issue with nearly every network.
- Who will perform maintenance?
- Degree of commitment and motivation to contribute.
- Periodic? On-demand as needed? Preventive?
- Equipment change-out schedules and upgrades for sensors and software.
- Automated stations require <u>skilled</u> and <u>experienced</u> labor.
- Calibration—sensors often drift (climate).
- Site maintenance essential (constant vegetation, surface conditions, nearby influences).
- Typical automated station will cost about $2K per year to maintain.
- Documentation—photos, notes, visits, changes, essential for posterity.
- Planning for equipment life cycle and technological advances.

C.7. Maintaining Programmatic Continuity and Corporate Knowledge
- Long-term vision and commitment needed.
- Institutionalizing versus personalizing—developing appropriate dependencies.

C.8. Data Flow
- Centralized ingest?
- Centralized access to data and data products?
- Local version available?
- Contract out work or do it yourself?
- Quality control of data.
- Archival.
- Metadata—historic information, not a snapshot. Every station should collect metadata.
- Post-collection processing, multiple data-ingestion paths.

C.9. Products
- Most basic product consists of the data values.
- Summaries.
- Write own applications or leverage existing mechanisms?

C.10. Funding
- Prototype approaches as proof of concept.
- Linking and leveraging essential.
- Constituencies—every network <u>needs</u> a constituency.
- Bridging to practical and operational communities? Live data needed.
- Bridging to counterpart research efforts and initiatives—funding source.
- Creativity, resourcefulness, and persistence usually are essential to success.

C.11. Final Comments
- Deployment is by far the easiest part in operating a network.
- Maintenance is the main issue.
- Best analogy: Operating a network is like raising a child; it requires constant attention.

Source: Western Regional Climate Center (WRCC)

Appendix D. Master metadata field list.

Field Name	Field Type	Field Description
begin_date	date	Effective beginning date for a record.
begin_date_flag	char(2)	Flag describing the known accuracy of the begin date for a station.
best_elevation	float(4)	Best known elevation for a station (in feet).
clim_div_code	char(2)	Foreign key defining climate division code (primary in table: clim_div).
clim_div_key	int2	Foreign key defining climate division for a station (primary in table: clim_div.
clim_div_name	varchar(30)	English name for a climate division.
controller_info	varchar(50)	Person or organization who maintains the identifier system for a given weather or climate network.
country_key	int2	Foreign key defining country where a station resides (primary in table: none).
county_key	int2	Foreign key defining county where a station resides (primary in table: county).
county_name	varchar(31)	English name for a county.
description	text	Any description pertaining to the particular table.
end_date	date	Last effective date for a record.
end_date_flag	char(2)	Flag describing the known accuracy of station end date.
fips_country_code	char(2)	FIPS (federal information processing standards) country code.
fips_state_abbr	char(2)	FIPS state abbreviation for a station.
fips_state_code	char(2)	FIPS state code for a station.
history_flag	char(2)	Describes temporal significance of an individual record among others from the same station.
id_type_key	int2	Foreign key defining the id_type for a station (usually defined in code).
last_updated	date	Date of last update for a record.
latitude	float(8)	Latitude value.
longitude	float(8)	Longitude value.
name_type_key	int2	"3": COOP station name, "2": best station name.
name	varchar(30)	Station name as known at date of last update entry.
ncdc_state_code	char(2)	NCDC, two-character code identifying U.S. state.
network_code	char(8)	Eight-character abbreviation code identifying a network.
network_key	int2	Foreign key defining the network for a station (primary in table: network).
network_station_id	int4	Identifier for a station in the associated network, which is defined by id_type_key.
remark	varchar(254)	Additional information for a record.
src_quality_code	char(2)	Code describing the data quality for the data source.
state_key	int2	Foreign key defining the U.S. state where a station resides (primary in table: state).
state_name	varchar(30)	English name for a state.
station_alt_name	varchar(30)	Other English names for a station.
station_best_name	varchar(30)	Best, most well-known English name for a station.
time_zone	float4	Time zone where a station resides.
ucan_station_id	int4	Unique station identifier for every station in ACIS.
unit_key	int2	Integer value representing a unit of measure.

Field Name	Field Type	Field Description
updated_by	char(8)	Person who last updated a record.
var_major_id	int2	Defines major climate variable.
var_minor_id	int2	Defines data source within a var_major_id.
zipcode	char(5)	Zipcode where a latitude/longitude point resides.
nps_netcode	char(4)	Network four-character identifier.
nps_netname	varchar(128)	Displayed English name for a network.
parkcode	char(4)	Park four-character identifier.
parkname	varchar(128)	Displayed English name for a park/
im_network	char(4)	NPS I&M network where park belongs (a net code)/
station_id	varchar(16)	Station identifier.
station_id_type	varchar(16)	Type of station identifier.
network.subnetwork.id	varchar(16)	Identifier of a sub-network in associated network.
subnetwork_key	int2	Foreign key defining sub-network for a station.
subnetwork_name	varchar(30)	English name for a sub-network.
slope	integer	Terrain slope at the location.
aspect	integer	Terrain aspect at the station.
gps	char(1)	Indicator of latitude/longitude recorded via GPS (global positioning system).
site_description	text(0)	Physical description of site.
route_directions	text(0)	Driving route or site access directions.
station_photo_id	integer	Unique identifier associating a group of photos to a station. Group of photos all taken on same date.
photo_id	char(30)	Unique identifier for a photo.
photo_date	datetime	Date photograph taken.
photographer	varchar(64)	Name of photographer.
maintenance_date	datetime	Date of station maintenance visit.
contact_key	Integer	Unique identifier associating contact information to a station.
full_name	varchar(64)	Full name of contact person.
organization	varchar(64)	Organization of contact person.
contact_type	varchar(32)	Type of contact person (operator, administrator, etc.)
position_title	varchar(32)	Title of contact person.
address	varchar(32)	Address for contact person.
city	varchar(32)	City for contact person.
state	varchar(2)	State for contact person.
zip_code	char(10)	Zipcode for contact person.
country	varchar(32)	Country for contact person.
email	varchar(64)	E-mail for contact person.
work_phone	varchar(16)	Work phone for contact person.
contact_notes	text(254)	Other details regarding contact person.
equipment_type	char(30)	Sensor measurement type; i.e., wind speed, air temperature, etc.
eq_manufacturer	char(30)	Manufacturer of equipment.
eq_model	char(20)	Model number of equipment.
serial_num	char(20)	Serial number of equipment.
eq_description	varchar(254)	Description of equipment.
install_date	datetime	Installation date of equipment.
remove_date	datetime	Removal date of equipment.
ref_height	integer	Sensor displacement height from surface.
sampling_interval	varchar(10)	Frequency of sensor measurement.

Appendix E. General design considerations for weather/ climate-monitoring programs.

The process for designing a climate-monitoring program benefits from anticipating design and protocol issues discussed here. Much of this material is been excerpted from a report addressing the Channel Islands National Park (Redmond and McCurdy 2005), where an example is found illustrating how these factors can be applied to a specific setting. Many national park units possess some climate or meteorology feature that sets them apart from more familiar or "standard" settings.

E.1. Introduction

There are several criteria that must be used in deciding to deploy new stations and where these new stations should be sited.
- Where are existing stations located?
- Where have data been gathered in the past (discontinued locations)?
- Where would a new station fill a knowledge gap about basic, long-term climatic averages for an area of interest?
- Where would a new station fill a knowledge gap about how climate behaves over time?
- As a special case for behavior over time, what locations might be expected to show a more sensitive response to climate change?
- How do answers to the preceding questions depend on the climate element? Are answers the same for precipitation, temperature, wind, snowfall, humidity, etc.?
- What role should manual measurements play? How should manual measurements interface with automated measurements?
- Are there special technical or management issues, either present or anticipated in the next 5–15 years, requiring added climate information?
- What unique information is provided in addition to information from existing sites? "Redundancy is bad."
- What nearby information is available to estimate missing observations because observing systems always experience gaps and lose data? "Redundancy is good."
- How would logistics and maintenance affect these decisions?

In relation to the preceding questions, there are several topics that should be considered. The following topics are not listed in a particular order.

E.1.1. Network Purpose

Humans seem to have an almost reflexive need to measure temperature and precipitation, along with other climate elements. These reasons span a broad range from utilitarian to curiosity-driven. Although there are well-known recurrent patterns of need and data use, new uses are always appearing. The number of uses ranges in the thousands. Attempts have been made to categorize such uses (see NRC 1998; NRC 2001). Because climate measurements are accumulated over a long time, they should be treated as multi-purpose and should be undertaken in a manner that serves the widest possible applications. Some applications remain constant, while others rise and fall in importance. An insistent issue today may subside, while the next pressing issue of tomorrow barely may be anticipated. The notion that humans might affect the climate of the entire Earth was nearly unimaginable when the national USDA (later NOAA) cooperative weather network began in the late 1800s. Abundant experience has shown, however, that there always will be a demand for a history record of climate measurements and their properties. Experience also shows that there is an expectation that climate measurements will be taken and made available to the general public.

An exhaustive list of uses for data would fill many pages and still be incomplete. In broad terms, however, there are needs to document environmental conditions that disrupt or otherwise affect park operations (e.g., storms and droughts). Design and construction standards are determined by climatological event frequencies that exceed certain thresholds. Climate is a determinant that sometimes attracts and sometimes discourages visitors. Climate may play a large part in the park experience (e.g., Death Valley and heat are nearly synonymous). Some park units are large enough to encompass spatial or elevation diversity in climate, and the sequence of events can vary considerably inside or close to park boundaries. That is, temporal trends and statistics may not be the same everywhere, and this spatial structure should be sampled. The granularity of this structure depends on the presence of topography or large climate gradients or both, such as that found along the U.S. West Coast in summer with the rapid transition from the marine layer to the hot interior.

Plant and animal communities and entire ecosystems react to every nuance in the physical environment. No aspect of weather and climate goes undetected in the natural world. Wilson (1998) proposed "an informal rule of biological evolution" that applies here: "If an organic sensor can be imagined that is capable of detecting any particular environmental signal, a species exists somewhere that possesses this sensor." Every weather and climate event, whether dull or extraordinary to humans, matters to some organism. Dramatic events and creeping incremental change both have consequences to living systems. Extreme events or disturbances can "reset the clock" or "shake up the system" and lead to reverberations that last for years to centuries or longer. Slow change can carry complex nonlinear systems (e.g., any living assemblage) into states where chaotic transitions and new behavior occur. These changes are seldom predictable, typically are observed after the fact, and understood only in retrospect. Climate changes may not be exciting, but as a well-known atmospheric scientist, Mike Wallace, from the University of Washington once noted, "subtle does not mean unimportant".

Thus, individuals who observe the climate should be able to record observations accurately and depict both rapid and slow changes. In particular, an array of artificial influences easily can confound detection of slow changes. The record as provided can contain both real climate variability (that took place in the atmosphere) and fake climate variability (that arose directly from the way atmospheric changes were observed and recorded). As an example, trees growing near a climate station with an excellent anemometer will make it appear that the wind gradually slowed down over many years. Great care must be taken to protect against sources of fake climate variability on the longer-time scales of years to decades. Processes leading to the observed climate are not stationary; rather these processes draw from probability distributions that vary with time. For this reason, climatic time series do not exhibit statistical stationarity. The implications are manifold. There are no true climatic "normals" to which climate inevitably must return. Rather, there are broad ranges of climatic conditions. Climate does not demonstrate exact repetition but instead continual fluctuation and sometimes approximate repetition. In addition, there is always new behavior waiting to occur. Consequently, the business of climate monitoring is never finished, and there is no point where we can state confidently that "enough" is known.

E.1.2. Robustness

The most frequent cause for loss of weather data is the weather itself, the very thing we wish to record. The design of climate and weather observing programs should consider the meteorological equivalent of "peaking power" employed by utilities. Because environmental disturbances have significant effects on ecologic systems, sensors, data loggers, and communications networks should be able to function during the most severe conditions that realistically can be anticipated over the next 50–100 years. Systems designed in this manner are less likely to fail under more ordinary conditions, as well as more likely to transmit continuous, quality data for both tranquil and active periods.

E.1.3. Weather versus Climate

For "weather" measurements, pertaining to what is approximately happening here and now, small moves and changes in exposure are not as critical. For "climate" measurements, where values from different points in time are compared, siting and exposure are critical factors, and it is vitally important that the observing circumstances remain essentially unchanged over the duration of the station record.

Station moves can affect different elements to differing degrees. Even small moves of several meters, especially vertically, can affect temperature records. Hills and knolls act differently from the bottoms of small swales, pockets, or drainage channels (Geiger et al. 2003; Whiteman 2000). Precipitation is probably less subject to change with moves of 50–100 m than other elements (that is, precipitation has less intrinsic variation in small spaces) except if wind flow over the gauge is affected.

E.1.4. Physical Setting

Siting and exposure, and their continuity and consistency through time, significantly influence the climate records produced by a station. These two terms have overlapping connotations. We use the term "siting" in a more general sense, reserving the term "exposure" generally for the particular circumstances affecting the ability of an instrument to record measurements that are representative of the desired spatial or temporal scale.

E.1.5. Measurement Intervals

Climatic processes occur continuously in time, but our measurement systems usually record in discrete chunks of time: for example, seconds, hours, or days. These measurements often are referred to as "systematic" measurements. Interval averages may hide active or interesting periods of highly intense activity. Alternatively, some systems record "events" when a certain threshold of activity is exceeded (examples: another millimeter of precipitation has fallen, another kilometer of wind has moved past, the temperature has changed by a degree, a gust higher than 9.9 m/s has been measured). When this occurs, measurements from all sensors are reported. These measurements are known as "breakpoint" data. In relatively unchanging conditions (long calm periods or rainless weeks, for example), event recorders should send a signal that they are still "alive and well." If systematic recorders are programmed to note and periodically report the highest, lowest, and mean value within each time interval, the likelihood is reduced that interesting behavior will be glossed over or lost. With the capacity of modern data loggers, it is recommended to record and report extremes within the basic time increment (e.g., hourly or 10 minutes). This approach also assists quality-control procedures.

There is usually a trade-off between data volume and time increment, and most automated systems now are set to record approximately hourly. A number of field stations maintained by WRCC are programmed to record in 5- or 10-minute increments, which readily serve to construct an hourly value. However, this approach produces 6–12 times as much data as hourly data. These systems typically do not record details of events at sub-interval time scales, but they easily can record peak values, or counts of threshold exceedance, within the time intervals.

Thus, for each time interval at an automated station, we recommend that several kinds of information—mean or sum, extreme maximum and minimum, and sometimes standard deviation—be recorded. These measurements are useful for quality control and other purposes. Modern data loggers and office computers have quite high capacity. Diagnostic information indicating the state of solar chargers or battery voltages and their extremes is of great value. This topic will be discussed in greater detail in a succeeding section.

Automation also has made possible adaptive or intelligent monitoring techniques where systems vary the recording rate based on detection of the behavior of interest by the software. Sub-interval behavior of interest can be masked on occasion (e.g., a 5-minute extreme downpour with high-erosive capability hidden by an innocuous hourly total). Most users prefer measurements that are systematic in time because they are much easier to summarize and manipulate.

For breakpoint data produced by event reporters, there also is a need to send periodically a signal that the station is still functioning, even though there is nothing more to report. "No report" does not necessarily mean "no data," and it is important to distinguish between the actual observation that was recorded and the content of that observation (e.g., an observation of "0.00" is not the same as "no observation").

E.1.6. Mixed Time Scales

There are times when we may wish to combine information from radically different scales. For example, over the past 100 years we may want to know how the frequency of 5-minute precipitation peaks has varied or how the frequency of peak 1-second wind gusts have varied. We may also want to know over this time if nearby vegetation gradually has grown up to increasingly block the wind or to slowly improve precipitation catch. Answers to these questions require knowledge over a wide range of time scales.

E.1.7. Elements

For manual measurements, the typical elements recorded included temperature extremes, precipitation, and snowfall/snow depth. Automated measurements typically include temperature, precipitation, humidity, wind speed and direction, and solar radiation. An exception to this exists in very windy locations where precipitation is difficult to measure accurately. Automated measurements of snow are improving, but manual measurements are still preferable, as long as shielding is present. Automated measurement of frozen precipitation presents numerous challenges that have not been resolved fully, and the best gauges are quite expensive ($3–8K). Soil temperatures also are included sometimes. Soil moisture is extremely useful, but measurements are not made at many sites. In addition, care must be taken in the installation and maintenance of instruments used in measuring soil moisture. Soil properties vary tremendously in short distances as well, and it is often very difficult ("impossible") to accurately document these variations (without digging up all the soil!). In cooler climates, ultrasonic sensors that detect snow depth are becoming commonplace.

E.1.8. Wind Standards

Wind varies the most in the shortest distance, since it always decreases to zero near the ground and increases rapidly (approximately logarithmically) with height near the ground. Changes in anemometer height obviously will affect distribution of wind speed as will changes in vegetation, obstructions such as buildings, etc. A site that has a 3-m (10-ft) mast clearly will be less windy than a site that has a 6-m (20-ft) or 10-m (33-ft) mast. Historically, many U.S. airports (FAA and NWS) and most current RAWS sites have used a standard 6-m (20-ft) mast for wind measurements. Some NPS RAWS sites utilize shorter masts. Over the last decade, as Automated Surface Observing Systems (ASOSs, mostly NWS) and Automated Weather Observing Systems (AWOSs, mostly FAA) have been deployed at most airports, wind masts have been raised to 8 or 10 m (26 or 33 ft), depending on airplane clearance. The World Meteorological Organization recommends 10 m as the height for wind measurements (WMO 1983; 2005), and more groups are migrating slowly to this standard. The American Association of State Climatologists (AASC 1985) have recommended that wind be measured at 3 m, a standard geared more for agricultural applications than for general purpose uses where higher levels usually are preferred. Different anemometers have different starting thresholds; therefore, areas that frequently experience very light winds may not produce wind measurements thus affecting long-term mean estimates of wind speed. For both sustained winds (averages over a short interval of 2–60 minutes) and especially for gusts, the duration of the sampling interval makes considerable difference. For the same wind history, 1–second gusts are higher than gusts averaging 3 seconds, which in turn are greater than 5-second averages, so that the same sequence would be described with different numbers (all three systems and more are in use). Changes in the averaging procedure, or in height or exposure, can lead to "false" or "fake" climate change with no change in actual climate. Changes in any of these should be noted in the metadata.

E.1.9. Wind Nomenclature

Wind is a vector quantity having a direction and a speed. Directions can be two- or three-dimensional; they will be three-dimensional if the vertical component is important. In all common uses, winds always are denoted by the direction they blow *from* (e.g., a north wind means the wind is coming from the north). This convention exists because wind often brings weather, and thus our attention is focused upstream. However, this approach contrasts with ocean currents, which usually are denoted by the direction they are moving *towards* (e.g., an eastward current moves from west to east). In specialized applications (such as in atmospheric modeling), wind velocity vectors point in the direction that the wind is blowing. Thus, a southwesterly wind (from the southwest) has both northward and eastward (to the north and to the east) components. Except near mountains, wind cannot blow up or down near the ground, so the vertical component of wind often is approximated as zero, and the horizontal component is emphasized.

E.1.10. Frozen Precipitation

Frozen precipitation is more difficult to measure than liquid precipitation, especially with automated techniques. Goodison et al. (1998), Sevruk and Harmon (1984), and Yang et al. (1998; 2001) provide many of the reasons to explain this. The importance of frozen precipitation varies greatly from one setting to another. This subject was discussed in greater detail in a related inventory and monitoring report for the Alaska park units (Redmond et al. 2005).

In climates that receive frozen precipitation, a decision must be made whether or not to try to record such events accurately. This usually means that the precipitation must be turned into liquid either by falling into an antifreeze fluid solution that is then weighed or by heating the precipitation enough to melt and fall through a measuring mechanism such as a nearly-balanced tipping bucket. Accurate measurements from the first approach require expensive gauges; tipping buckets can achieve this resolution readily but are more apt to lose some or all precipitation. Improvements have been made to the heating mechanism on the NWS tipping-bucket gauge used for the ASOS to correct its numerous deficiencies making it less problematic; however, this gauge is not inexpensive. A heat supply needed to melt frozen precipitation usually requires more energy than renewable energy (solar panels or wind recharging) can provide thus AC power is needed. The availability of AC power is severely limited in many cold or remote U. S. settings. Furthermore, periods of frozen precipitation or rime often provide less-than-optimal recharging conditions with heavy clouds, short days, low-solar-elevation angles and more horizon blocking, and cold temperatures causing additional drain on the battery.

E.1.11. Save or Lose

A second consideration with precipitation is determining if the measurement should be saved (as in weighing systems) or lost (as in tipping-bucket systems). With tipping buckets, after the water has passed through the tipping mechanism, it usually just drops to the ground. Thus, there is no checksum to ensure that the sum of all the tips adds up to what has been saved in a reservoir at some location. By contrast, the weighing gauges continually accumulate until the reservoir is emptied, the reported value is the total reservoir content (for example, the height of the liquid column in a tube), and the incremental precipitation is the difference in depth between two known times. These weighing gauges do not always have the same fine resolution. Some gauges only record to the nearest centimeter, which is usually acceptable for hydrology but not necessarily for other needs. (For reference, a millimeter of precipitation can get a person in street clothes quite wet.) This is how the NRCS/USDA SNOTEL system works in climates that measure up to 3000 cm of snow in a winter. (See http://www.wcc.nrcs.usda.gov/publications for publications or http://www.wcc.nrcs.usda.gov/factpub/aib536.html for a specific description.) No precipitation is lost this way. A thin layer of oil is used to suppress evaporation, and anti-freeze ensures that frozen precipitation melts. When initially recharged, the sum of the oil and starting antifreeze solution is treated as the zero point. The anti-freeze usually is not sufficiently environmentally friendly to discharge to the ground and thus must be hauled into the area and then back out. Other weighing gauges are capable of measuring to the 0.25-mm (0.01-in.) resolution but do not have as much capacity and must be emptied more often. Day/night and storm-related thermal expansion and contraction and sometimes wind shaking can cause fluid pressure from accumulated totals to go up and down in SNOTEL gauges by small increments (commonly 0.3-3 cm, or 0.01–0.10 ft) leading to "negative precipitation" followed by similarly non-real light precipitation when, in fact, no change took place in the amount of accumulated precipitation.

E.1.12. Time

Time should always be in local standard time (LST), and daylight savings time (DST) should never be used under any circumstances with automated equipment and timers. Using DST leads to one duplicate hour, one missing hour, and a season of displaced values, as well as needless confusion and a data-management nightmare. Absolute time, such as Greenwich Mean Time (GMT) or Coordinated Universal Time (UTC), also can be used because these formats are unambiguously translatable. Since measurements only provide information about what already *has* occurred or *is* occurring and not what *will* occur, they should always be assigned to the *ending time* of the associated interval with hour 24 marking the end of the last hour of the day. In this system, midnight always represents the end of the day, not the start. To demonstrate the importance of this differentiation, we have encountered situations where police officers seeking corroborating weather data could not recall whether the time on their crime report from a year ago was the starting midnight or the ending midnight! Station positions should be known to within a few meters, easily accomplished with GPS, so that time zones and solar angles can be determined accurately.

E.1.13. Automated versus Manual

Most of this report has addressed automated measurements. Historically, most measurements are manual and typically collected once a day. In many cases, manual measurements continue because of habit, usefulness, and desire for continuity over time. Manual measurements are extremely useful and when possible should be encouraged. However, automated measurements are becoming more common. For either, it is important to record time in a logically consistent manner.

It should not be automatically assumed that newer data and measurements are "better" than older data or that manual data are "worse" than automated data. Older or simpler manual measurements are often of very high quality even if they sometimes are not in the most convenient digital format.

There is widespread desire to use automated systems to reduce human involvement. This is admirable and understandable, but every automated weather/climate station or network requires significant human attention and maintenance. A telling example concerns the Oklahoma Mesonet (see Brock et al. 1995, and bibliography at http://www.mesonet.ou.edu), a network of about 115 high–quality, automated meteorological stations spread over Oklahoma, where about 80 percent of the annual ($2–3M) budget is nonetheless allocated to humans with only about 20 percent allocated to equipment.

E.1.14. Manual Conventions

Manual measurements typically are made once a day. Elements usually consist of maximum and minimum temperature, temperature at observation time, precipitation, snowfall, snow depth, and sometimes evaporation, wind, or other information. Since it is not actually known when extremes occurred, the only logical approach, and the nationwide convention, is to ascribe the entire measurement to the time-interval date and to enter it on the form in that way. For morning observers (for example, 8 am to 8 am), this means that the maximum temperature written for today often is from yesterday afternoon and sometimes the minimum temperature for the 24-hr period actually occurred yesterday morning. However, this is understood and expected. It is often a surprise to observers to see how many maximum temperatures do not occur in the afternoon and how many minimum temperatures do not occur in the predawn hours. This is especially true in environments that are colder, higher, northerly, cloudy, mountainous, or coastal. As long as this convention is strictly followed every day, it has been shown that truly excellent climate records can result (Redmond 1992). Manual observers should reset equipment only one time per day at the official observing time. Making more than one measurement a day is discouraged strongly; this practice results in a hybrid record that is too difficult to interpret. The only exception is for total daily snowfall. New snowfall can be measured up to four times per day with no observations closer than six hours. It is well known that more frequent measurement of snow increases the annual total because compaction is a continuous process.

Two main purposes for climate observations are to establish the long-term averages for given locations and to track variations in climate. Broadly speaking, these purposes address topics of absolute and relative climate behavior. Once absolute behavior has been "established" (a task that is never finished because long-term averages continue to vary in time)—temporal variability quickly becomes the item of most interest.

E.2. Representativeness

Having discussed important factors to consider when new sites are installed, we now turn our attention to site "representativeness." In popular usage, we often encounter the notion that a site is "representative" of another site if it receives the same annual precipitation or records the same annual temperature or if some other element-specific, long-term average has a similar value. This notion of representativeness has a certain limited validity, but there are other aspects of this idea that need to be considered.

A climate monitoring site also can be said to be representative if climate records from that site show sufficiently strong temporal correlations with a large number of locations over a sufficiently large area. If station A receives 20 cm a year and station B receives 200 cm a year, these climates obviously receive quite differing amounts of precipitation. However, if their monthly, seasonal, or annual correlations are high (for example, 0.80 or higher for a particular time scale), one site can be used as a surrogate for estimating values at the other if measurements for a particular month, season, or year are missing. That is, a wet or dry month at one station is also a wet or dry month (relative to its own mean) at the comparison station. Note that high correlations on one time scale do not imply automatically that high correlations will occur on other time scales.

Likewise, two stations having similar mean climates (for example, similar annual precipitation) might not co-vary in close synchrony (for example, coastal versus interior). This may be considered a matter of climate "affiliation" for a particular location.

Thus, the representativeness of a site can refer either to the basic climatic averages for a given duration (or time window within the annual cycle) or to the extent that the site co-varies in time with respect to all surrounding locations. One site can be representative of another in the first sense but not the second, or vice versa, or neither, or both—all combinations are possible.

If two sites are perfectly correlated then, in a sense, they are "redundant." However, redundancy has value because all sites will experience missing data especially with automated equipment in rugged environments and harsh climates where outages and other problems nearly can be guaranteed. In many cases, those outages are caused by the weather, particularly by unusual weather and the very conditions we most wish to know about. Methods for filling in those values will require proxy information from this or other nearby networks. Thus, redundancy is a virtue rather than a vice.

In general, the cooperative stations managed by the NWS have produced much longer records than automated stations like RAWS or SNOTEL stations. The RAWS stations often have problems with precipitation, especially in winter, or with missing data, so that low correlations may be data problems rather than climatic dissimilarity. The RAWS records also are relatively short, so correlations should be interpreted with care. In performing and interpreting such analyses, however, we must remember that there are physical climate reasons and observational reasons why stations within a short distance (even a few tens or hundreds of meters) may not correlate well.

E.2.1. Temporal Behavior

It is possible that high correlations will occur between station pairs during certain portions of the year (i.e., January) but low correlations may occur during other portions of the year (e.g., September or October). The relative contributions of these seasons to the annual total (for precipitation) or average (for temperature) and the correlations for each month are both factors in the correlation of an aggregated time window of longer duration that encompasses those seasons (e.g., one of the year definitions such as calendar year or water year). A complete and careful evaluation ideally would include such a correlation analysis but requires more resources and data. Note that it also is possible and frequently is observed that temperatures are highly correlated while precipitation is not or vice versa, and these relations can change according to the time of year. If two stations are well correlated for all climate elements for all portions of the year, then they can be considered redundant.

With scarce resources, the initial strategy should be to try to identify locations that do not correlate particularly well, so that each new site measures something new that cannot be guessed easily from the behavior of surrounding sites. (An important caveat here is that lack of such correlation could be a result of physical climate behavior and not a result of faults with the actual measuring process; i.e., by unrepresentative or simply poor-quality data. Unfortunately, we seldom have perfect climate data.) As additional sites are added, we usually wish for some combination of unique and redundant sites to meet what amounts to essentially orthogonal constraints: new information and more reliably-furnished information.

A common consideration is whether to observe on a ridge or in a valley, given the resources to place a single station within a particular area of a few square kilometers. Ridge and valley stations will correlate very well for temperatures when lapse conditions prevail, particularly summer daytime temperatures. In summer at night or winter at daylight, the picture will be more mixed and correlations will be lower. In winter at night when inversions are common and even the rule, correlations may be zero or even negative and perhaps even more divergent as the two sites are on opposite sides of the inversion. If we had the luxury of locating stations everywhere, we would find that ridge tops generally correlate very well with other ridge tops and similarly valleys with other valleys, but ridge tops correlate well with valleys only under certain circumstances. Beyond this, valleys and ridges having similar orientations usually will correlate better with each other than those with perpendicular orientations, depending on their orientation with respect to large-scale wind flow and solar angles.

Unfortunately, we do not have stations everywhere, so we are forced to use the few comparisons that we have and include a large dose of intelligent reasoning, using what we have observed elsewhere. In performing and interpreting such analyses, we must remember that there are physical climatic reasons and observational reasons why stations within a short distance (even a few tens or hundreds of meters) may not correlate well.

Examples of correlation analyses include those for the Channel Islands and for southwest Alaska, which can be found in Redmond and McCurdy (2005) and Redmond et al. (2005). These examples illustrate what can be learned from correlation analyses. Spatial correlations generally vary by time of year. Thus, results should be displayed in the form of annual correlation cycles— for monthly mean temperature and monthly total precipitation and perhaps other climate elements like wind or humidity—between station pairs selected for climatic setting and data availability and quality.

In general, the COOP stations managed by the NWS have produced much longer records than have automated stations like RAWS or SNOTEL stations. The RAWS stations also often have problems with precipitation, especially in winter or with missing data, so that low correlations may be data problems rather than climate dissimilarity. The RAWS records are much shorter, so correlations should be interpreted with care, but these stations are more likely to be in places of interest for remote or under-sampled regions.

E.2.2. Spatial Behavior

A number of techniques exist to interpolate from isolated point values to a spatial domain. For example, a common technique is simple inverse distance weighting. Critical to the success of the simplest of such techniques is that some other property of the spatial domain, one that is influential for the mapped element, does not vary significantly. Topography greatly influences precipitation, temperature, wind, humidity, and most other meteorological elements. Thus, this criterion clearly is not met in any region having extreme topographic diversity. In such circumstances, simple Cartesian distance may have little to do with how rapidly correlation deteriorates from one site to the next, and in fact, the correlations can decrease readily from a mountain to a valley and then increase again on the next mountain. Such structure in the fields of spatial correlation is not seen in the relatively (statistically) well-behaved flat areas like those in the eastern United States.

To account for dominating effects such as topography and inland–coastal differences that exist in certain regions, some kind of additional knowledge must be brought to bear to produce meaningful, physically plausible, and observationally based interpolations. Historically, this has proven to be an extremely difficult problem, especially to perform objective and repeatable analyses. An analysis performed for southwest Alaska (Redmond et al. 2005) concluded that the PRISM (Parameter Regression on Independent Slopes Model) maps (Daly et al. 1994; 2002; Gibson et al. 2002; Doggett et al. 2004) were probably the best available. An analysis by Simpson et al. (2005) further discussed many issues in the mapping of Alaska's climate and resulted in the same conclusion about PRISM.

E.2.3. Climate-Change Detection

Although general purpose climate stations should be situated to address all aspects of climate variability, it is desirable that they also be in locations that are more sensitive to climate change from natural or anthropogenic influences should it begin to occur. The question here is how well we know such sensitivities. The polar regions and especially the North Pole are generally regarded as being more sensitive to changes in radiative forcing of climate because of positive feedbacks. The climate-change issue is quite complex because it encompasses more than just greenhouse gasses.

Sites that are in locations or climates particularly vulnerable to climate change should be favored. How this vulnerability is determined is a considerably challenging research issue. Candidate locations or situations are those that lie on the border between two major biomes or just inside the edge of one or the other. In these cases, a slight movement of the boundary in anticipated direction (toward "warmer," for example) would be much easier to detect as the boundary moves past the site and a different set of biota begin to be established. Such a vegetative or ecologic response would be more visible and would take less time to establish as a real change than would a smaller change in the center of the distribution range of a marker or key species.

E.2.4. Element-Specific Differences

The various climate elements (temperature, precipitation, cloudiness, snowfall, humidity, wind speed and direction, solar radiation) do not vary through time in the same sequence or manner nor should they necessarily be expected to vary in this manner. The spatial patterns of variability should not be expected to be the same for all elements. These patterns also should not be expected to be similar for all months or seasons. The suitability of individual sites for measurement also varies from one element to another. A site that has a favorable exposure for temperature or wind may not have a favorable exposure for precipitation or snowfall. A site that experiences proper air movement may be situated in a topographic channel, such as a river valley or a pass, which restricts the range of wind directions and affects the distribution of speed-direction categories.

E.2.5. Logistics and Practical Factors

Even with the most advanced scientific rationale, sites in some remote or climatically challenging settings may not be suitable because of the difficulty in servicing and maintaining equipment. Contributing to these challenges are scheduling difficulties, animal behavior, snow burial, icing, snow behavior, access and logistical problems, and the weather itself. Remote and elevated sites usually require far more attention and expense than a rain-dominated, easily accessible valley location.

For climate purposes, station exposure and the local environment should be maintained in their original state (vegetation especially), so that changes seen are the result of regional climate variations and not of trees growing up, bushes crowding a site, surface albedo changing, fire clearing, etc. Repeat photography has shown many examples of slow environmental change in the vicinity of a station in rather short time frames (5–20 years), and this technique should be employed routinely and frequently at all locations. In the end, logistics, maintenance, and other practical factors almost always determine the success of weather- and climate-monitoring activities.

E.2.6. Personnel Factors

Many past experiences (almost exclusively negative) strongly support the necessity to place primary responsibility for station deployment and maintenance in the hands of seasoned, highly qualified, trained, and meticulously careful personnel, the more experienced the better. Over time, even in "benign" climates but especially where harsher conditions prevail, every conceivable problem will occur and both the usual and unusual should be anticipated: weather, animals, plants, salt, sensor and communication failure, windblown debris, corrosion, power failures, vibrations, avalanches, snow loading and creep, corruption of the data logger program, etc. An ability to anticipate and forestall such problems, a knack for innovation and improvisation, knowledge of electronics, practical and organizational skills, and presence of mind to bring the various small but vital parts, spares, tools, and diagnostic troubleshooting equipment are highly valued qualities. Especially when logistics are so expensive, a premium should be placed on using experienced personnel, since the slightest and seemingly most minor mistake can render a station useless or, even worse, uncertain. Exclusive reliance on individuals without this background can be costly and almost always will result eventually in unnecessary loss of data. Skilled labor and an apprenticeship system to develop new skilled labor will greatly reduce (but not eliminate) the types of problems that can occur in operating a climate network.

E.3. Site Selection

In addition to considerations identified previously in this appendix, various factors need to be considered in selecting sites for new or augmented instrumentation.

E.3.1. Equipment and Exposure Factors

E.3.1.1. Measurement Suite: All sites should measure temperature, humidity, wind, solar radiation, and snow depth. Precipitation measurements are more difficult but probably should be attempted with the understanding that winter measurements may be of limited or no value unless an all-weather gauge has been installed. Even if an all-weather gauge has been installed, it is desirable to have a second gauge present that operates on a different principle–for example, a fluid-based system like those used in the SNOTEL stations in tandem with a higher–resolution, tipping bucket gauge for summertime. Without heating, a tipping bucket gauge usually is of use only when temperatures are above freezing and when temperatures have not been below freezing for some time, so that accumulated ice and snow is not melting and being recorded as present precipitation. Gauge undercatch is a significant issue in snowy climates, so shielding should be considered for all gauges designed to work over the winter months. It is very important to note the presence or absence of shielding, the type of shielding, and the dates of installation or removal of the shielding.

E.3.1.2. Overall Exposure: The ideal, general all-purpose site has gentle slopes, is open to the sun and the wind, has a natural vegetative cover, avoids strong local (less than 200 m) influences, and represents a reasonable compromise among all climate elements. The best temperature sites are not the best precipitation sites, and the same is true for other elements. Steep topography in the immediate vicinity should be avoided unless settings where precipitation is affected by steep topography are being deliberately sought or a mountaintop or ridgeline is the desired location. The potential for disturbance should be considered: fire and flood risk, earth movement, wind-borne debris, volcanic deposits or lahars, vandalism, animal tampering, and general human encroachment are all factors.

E.3.1.3. Elevation: Mountain climates do not vary in time in exactly the same manner as adjoining valley climates. This concept is emphasized when temperature inversions are present to a greater degree and during precipitation when winds rise up the slopes at the same angle. There is considerable concern that mountain climates will be (or already are) changing and perhaps changing differently than lowland climates, which has direct and indirect consequences for plant and animal life in the more extreme zones. Elevations of special significance are those that are near the mean rain/snow line for winter, near the tree line, and near the mean annual freezing level (all of these may not be quite the same). Because the lapse rates in wet climates often are nearly moist-adiabatic during the main precipitation seasons, measurements at one elevation may be extrapolated to nearby elevations. In drier climates and in the winter, temperature and to a lesser extent wind will show various elevation profiles.

E.3.1.4. Transects: The concept of observing transects that span climatic gradients is sound. This is not always straightforward in topographically uneven terrain, but these transects could still be arranged by setting up station(s) along the coast; in or near passes atop the main coastal interior drainage divide; and inland at one, two, or three distances into the interior lowlands. Transects need not—and by dint of topographic constraints probably cannot—be straight lines, but the closer that a line can be approximated the better. The main point is to systematically sample the key points of a behavioral transition without deviating too radically from linearity.

E.3.1.5. Other Topographic Considerations: There are various considerations with respect to local topography. Local topography can influence wind (channeling, upslope/downslope, etc.), precipitation (orographic enhancement, downslope evaporation, catch efficiency, etc.), and temperature (frost pockets, hilltops, aspect, mixing or decoupling from the overlying atmosphere, bowls, radiative effects, etc.), to different degrees at differing scales. In general, for measurements to be areally representative, it is better to avoid these local effects to the extent that they can be identified before station deployment (once deployed, it is desirable not to move a station). The primary purpose of a climate-monitoring network should be to serve as an infrastructure in the form of a set of benchmark stations for comparing other stations. Sometimes, however, it is exactly these local phenomena that we want to capture. Living organisms, especially plants, are affected by their immediate environment, whether it is representative of a larger setting or not. Specific measurements of limited scope and duration made for these purposes then can be tied to the main benchmarks. This experience is useful also in determining the complexity needed in the benchmark monitoring process in order to capture particular phenomena at particular space and time scales.

Sites that drain (cold air) well generally are better than sites that allow cold air to pool. Slightly sloped areas (1 degree is fine) or small benches from tens to hundreds of meters above streams are often favorable locations. Furthermore, these sites often tend to be out of the path of hazards (like floods) and to have rocky outcroppings where controlling vegetation will not be a major concern. Benches or wide spots on the rise between two forks of a river system are often the only flat areas and sometimes jut out to give greater exposure to winds from more directions.

E.3.1.6. Prior History: The starting point in designing a program is to determine what kinds of observations have been collected over time, by whom, in what manner, and if these observation are continuing to the present time. It also may be of value to "re-occupy" the former site of a station that is now inactive to provide some measure of continuity or a reference point from the past. This can be of value even if continuous observations were not made during the entire intervening period.

E.3.2. Element-Specific Factors

E.3.2.1. Temperature: An open exposure with uninhibited air movement is the preferred setting. The most common measurement is made at approximately eye level, 1.5–2.0 m. In snowy locations sensors should be at least one meter higher than the deepest snowpack expected in the next 50 years or perhaps 2–3 times the depth of the average maximum annual depth. Sensors should be shielded above and below from solar radiation (bouncing off snow), from sunrise/sunset horizontal input, and from vertical rock faces. Sensors should be clamped tightly, so that they do not swivel away from level stacks of radiation plates. Nearby vegetation should be kept away from the sensors (several meters). Growing vegetation should be cut to original conditions. Small hollows and swales can cool tremendously at night, and it is best avoid these areas. Side slopes of perhaps a degree or two of angle facilitate air movement and drainage and, in effect, sample a large area during nighttime hours. The very bottom of a valley should be avoided. Temperature can change substantially from moves of only a few meters. Situations have been observed where flat and seemingly uniform conditions (like airport runways) appear to demonstrate different climate behaviors over short distances of a few tens or hundreds of meters (differences of 5–10°C). When snow is on the ground, these microclimatic differences can be stronger, and differences of 2–5°C can occur in the short distance between the thermometer and the snow surface on calm evenings.

E.3.2.2. Precipitation (liquid): Calm locations with vegetative or artificial shielding are preferred. Wind will adversely impact readings; therefore, the less the better. Wind effects on precipitation are far less for rain than for snow. Devices that "save" precipitation present advantages, but most gauges are built to dump precipitation as it falls or to empty periodically. Automated gauges give both the amount and the timing. Simple backups that record only the total precipitation since the last visit have a certain advantage (for example, storage gauges or lengths of PVC pipe perhaps with bladders on the bottom). The following question should be asked: Does the total precipitation from an automated gauge add up to the measured total in a simple bucket (evaporation is prevented with an appropriate substance such as mineral oil)? Drip from overhanging foliage and trees can augment precipitation totals.

E.3.2.3. Precipitation (frozen): Calm locations or shielding are a must. Undercatch for rain is only about 5 percent, but with winds of only 2–4 m/s, gauges may catch only 30–70 percent of the actual snow falling depending on density of the flakes. To catch 100 percent of the snow, the standard configuration for shielding is employed by the CRN (Climate Reference Network): the DFIR (Double-Fence Intercomparison Reference) shield with 2.4-m (8-ft.) vertical, wooden slatted fences in two concentric octagons with diameters of 8 m and 4 m (26 ft and 13 ft, respectively) and an inner Alter shield (flapping vanes). Numerous tests have shown this is the only way to achieve complete catch of snowfall (e.g., Yang et al. 1998; 2001). The DFIR shield is large and bulky; it is recommended that all precipitation gauges have at least Alter shields on them.

Near the coast, much snow is heavy and falls more vertically. In colder locations or storms, light flakes frequently will fly in and then out of the gauge. Clearings in forests are usually excellent sites. Snow blowing from trees that are too close can augment actual precipitation totals. Artificial shielding (vanes, etc.) placed around gauges in snowy locales always should be used if accurate totals are desired. Moving parts tend to freeze up. Capping of gauges during heavy snowfall events is a common occurrence. When the cap becomes pointed, snow falls off to the ground and is not recorded. Caps and plugs often will not fall into the tube until hours, days, or even weeks have passed, typically during an extended period of freezing temperature or above or when sunlight finally occurs. Liquid-based measurements (e.g., SNOTEL "rocket" gauges) do not have the resolution (usually 0.3 cm [0.1 in.] rather than 0.03 cm [0.01 in.]) that tipping bucket and other gauges have but are known to be reasonably accurate in very snowy climates. Light snowfall events might not be recorded until enough of them add up to the next reporting increment. More expensive gauges like Geonors can be considered and could do quite well in snowy settings; however, they need to be emptied every 40 cm (15 in.) or so (capacity of 51 cm [20 in.]) until the new 91-cm (36-in.) capacity gauge is offered for sale. Recently, the NWS has been trying out the new (and very expensive) Ott all-weather gauge. Riming can be an issue in windy foggy environments below freezing. Rime, dew, and other forms of atmospheric condensation are not real precipitation, since they are caused by the gauge.

E.3.2.4. Snow Depth: Windswept areas tend to be blown clear of snow. Conversely, certain types of vegetation can act as a snow fence and cause artificial drifts. However, some amount of vegetation in the vicinity generally can help slow down the wind. The two most common types of snow-depth gauges are the Judd Snow Depth Sensor, produced by Judd Communications, and the snow depth gauge produced by Campbell Scientific, Inc. Opinions vary on which one is better. These gauges use ultrasound and look downward in a cone about 22 degrees in diameter. The ground should be relatively clear of vegetation and maintained in a manner so that the zero point on the calibration scale does not change.

E.3.2.5. Snow Water Equivalent: This is determined by the weight of snow on fluid-filled pads about the size of a desktop set up sometimes in groups of four or in larger hexagons several meters in diameter. These pads require flat ground some distance from nearby sources of windblown snow and shielding that is "just right": not too close to the shielding to act as a kind of snow fence and not too far from the shielding so that blowing and drifting become a factor. Generally, these pads require fluids that possess antifreeze-like properties, as well as handling and replacement protocols.

E.3.2.6. Wind: Open exposures are needed for wind measurements. Small prominences or benches without blockage from certain sectors are preferred. A typical rule for trees is to site stations back 10 tree-heights from all tree obstructions. Sites in long, narrow valleys can obviously only exhibit two main wind directions. Gently rounded eminences are more favored. Any kind of topographic steering should be avoided to the extent possible. Avoiding major mountain chains or single isolated mountains or ridges is usually a favorable approach, if there is a choice. Sustained wind speed and the highest gusts (1-second) should be recorded. Averaging methodologies for both sustained winds and gusts can affect climate trends and should be recorded as metadata with all changes noted. Vegetation growth affects the vertical wind profile, and growth over a few years can lead to changes in mean wind speed even if the "real" wind does not change, so vegetation near the site (perhaps out to 50 m) should be maintained in a quasi-permanent status (same height and spatial distribution). Wind devices can rime up and freeze or spin out of balance. In severely rimed or windy climates, rugged anemometers, such as those made by Taylor, are worth considering. These anemometers are expensive but durable and can withstand substantial abuse. In exposed locations, personnel should plan for winds to be at least 50 m/s and be able to measure these wind speeds. At a minimum, anemometers should be rated to 75 m/s.

E.3.2.7. Humidity: Humidity is a relatively straightforward climate element. Close proximity to lakes or other water features can affect readings. Humidity readings typically are less accurate near 100 percent and at low humidities in cold weather.

E.3.2.8. Solar Radiation: A site with an unobstructed horizon obviously is the most desirable. This generally implies a flat plateau or summit. However, in most locations trees or mountains will obstruct the sun for part of the day.

E.3.2.9. Soil Temperature: It is desirable to measure soil temperature at locations where soil is present. If soil temperature is recorded at only a single depth, the most preferred depth is 10 cm. Other common depths include 25 cm, 50 cm, 2 cm, and 100 cm. Biological activity in the soil will be proportional to temperature with important threshold effects occurring near freezing.

E.3.2.10. Soil Moisture: Soil-moisture gauges are somewhat temperamental and require care to install. The soil should be characterized by a soil expert during installation of the gauge. The readings may require a certain level of experience to interpret correctly. If accurate, readings of soil moisture are especially useful.

E.3.2.11. Distributed Observations: It can be seen readily that compromises must be struck among the considerations described in the preceding paragraphs because some are mutually exclusive.

How large can a "site" be? Generally, the equipment footprint should be kept as small as practical with all components placed next to each other (within less than 10–20 m or so). Readings from one instrument frequently are used to aid in interpreting readings from the remaining instruments.

What is a tolerable degree of separation? Some consideration may be given to locating a precipitation gauge or snow pillow among protective vegetation, while the associated temperature, wind, and humidity readings would be collected more effectively in an open and exposed location within 20–50 m. Ideally, it is advantageous to know the wind measurement precisely at the precipitation gauge, but a compromise involving a short split, and in effect a "distributed observation," could be considered. There are no definitive rules governing this decision, but it is suggested that the site footprint be kept within approximately 50 m. There also are constraints imposed by engineering and electrical factors that affect cable lengths, signal strength, and line noise; therefore, the shorter the cable the better. Practical issues include the need to trench a channel to outlying instruments or to allow lines to lie atop the ground and associated problems with animals, humans, weathering, etc. Separating a precipitation gauge up to 100 m or so from an instrument mast may be an acceptable compromise if other factors are not limiting.

E.3.2.12. Instrument Replacement Schedules: Instruments slowly degrade, and a plan for replacing them with new, refurbished, or recalibrated instruments should be in place. After approximately five years, a systematic change-out procedure should result in replacing most sensors in a network. Certain parts, such as solar radiation sensors, are candidates for annual calibration or change-out. Anemometers tend to degrade as bearings erode or electrical contacts become uneven. Noisy bearings are an indication, and a stethoscope might aid in hearing such noises. Increased internal friction affects the threshold starting speed; once spinning, they tend to function properly. Increases in starting threshold speeds can lead to more zero-wind measurements and thus reduce the reported mean wind speed with no real change in wind properties. A field calibration kit should be developed and taken on all site visits, routine or otherwise. Rain gauges can be tested with drip testers during field visits. Protective conduit and tight water seals can prevent abrasion and moisture problems with the equipment, although seals can keep moisture in as well as out. Bulletproof casings sometimes are employed in remote settings. A supply of spare parts, at least one of each and more for less-expensive or more-delicate sensors, should be maintained to allow replacement of worn or nonfunctional instruments during field visits. In addition, this approach allows instruments to be calibrated in the relative convenience of the operational home—the larger the network, the greater the need for a parts depot.

E.3.3. Long-Term Comparability and Consistency

E.3.3.1. Consistency: The emphasis here is to hold biases constant. Every site has biases, problems, and idiosyncrasies of one sort or another. The best rule to follow is simply to try to keep biases constant through time. Since the goal is to track climate through time, keeping sensors, methodologies, and exposure constant will ensure that only true climate change is being measured. This means leaving the site in its original state or performing maintenance to keep it that way. Once a site is installed, the goal should be to never move the site even by a few meters or to allow significant changes to occur within 100 m for the next several decades.

Sites in or near rock outcroppings likely will experience less vegetative disturbance or growth through the years and will not usually retain moisture, a factor that could speed corrosion. Sites that will remain locally similar for some time are usually preferable. However, in some cases the intent of a station might be to record the local climate effects of changes within a small-scale system (for example, glacier, recently burned area, or scene of some other disturbance) that is subject to a regional climate influence. In this example, the local changes might be much larger than the regional changes.

E.3.3.2. Metadata: Since the climate of every site is affected by features in the immediate vicinity, it is vital to record this information over time and to update the record repeatedly at each service visit. Distances, angles, heights of vegetation, fine-scale topography, condition of instruments, shielding discoloration, and other factors from within a meter to several kilometers should be noted. Systematic photography should be undertaken and updated at least once every one–two years.

Photographic documentation should be taken at each site in a standard manner and repeated every two–three years. Guidelines for methodology were developed by Redmond (2004) as a result of experience with the NOAA CRN and can be found on the WRCC NPS Web pages at http://www.wrcc.dri.edu/nps and at ftp://ftp.wrcc.dri.edu/nps/photodocumentation.pdf.

The main purpose for climate stations is to *track climatic conditions through time*. Anything that affects the interpretation of records through time must to be noted and recorded for posterity. The important factors should be clear to a person who has never visited the site, no matter how long ago the site was installed.

In regions with significant, climatic transition zones, transects are an efficient way to span several climates and make use of available resources. Discussions on this topic at greater detail can be found in Redmond and Simeral (2004) and in Redmond et al. (2005).

E.4. Literature Cited

American Association of State Climatologists. 1985. Heights and exposure standards for sensors on automated weather stations. The State Climatologist **9**.

Brock, F. V., K. C. Crawford, R. L. Elliott, G. W. Cuperus, S. J. Stadler, H. L. Johnson and M. D. Eilts. 1995. The Oklahoma Mesonet: A technical overview. Journal of Atmospheric and Oceanic Technology **12**:5-19.

Daly, C., R. P. Neilson, and D. L. Phillips. 1994. A statistical-topographic model for mapping climatological precipitation over mountainous terrain. Journal of Applied Meteorology **33**:140-158.

Daly, C., W. P. Gibson, G. H. Taylor, G. L. Johnson, and P. Pasteris. 2002. A knowledge-based approach to the statistical mapping of climate. Climate Research **22**:99-113.

Doggett, M., C. Daly, J. Smith, W. Gibson, G. Taylor, G. Johnson, and P. Pasteris. 2004. High-resolution 1971-2000 mean monthly temperature maps for the western United States. Fourteenth AMS Conf. on Applied Climatology, 84th AMS Annual Meeting. Seattle, WA, American Meteorological Society, Boston, MA, January 2004, Paper 4.3, CD-ROM.

Geiger, R., R. H. Aron, and P. E. Todhunter. 2003. The Climate Near the Ground. 6th edition. Rowman & Littlefield Publishers, Inc., New York.

Gibson, W. P., C. Daly, T. Kittel, D. Nychka, C. Johns, N. Rosenbloom, A. McNab, and G. Taylor. 2002. Development of a 103-year high-resolution climate data set for the conterminous United States. Thirteenth AMS Conf. on Applied Climatology. Portland, OR, American Meteorological Society, Boston, MA, May 2002:181-183.

Goodison, B. E., P. Y. T. Louie, and D. Yang. 1998. WMO solid precipitation measurement intercomparison final report. WMO TD 982, World Meteorological Organization, Geneva, Switzerland.

National Research Council. 1998. Future of the National Weather Service Cooperative Weather Network. National Academies Press, Washington, D.C.

National Research Council. 2001. A Climate Services Vision: First Steps Toward the Future. National Academies Press, Washington, D.C.

Redmond, K. T. 1992. Effects of observation time on interpretation of climatic time series - A need for consistency. Eighth Annual Pacific Climate (PACLIM) Workshop. Pacific Grove, CA, March 1991:141-150.

Redmond, K. T. 2004. Photographic documentation of long-term climate stations. Available from ftp://ftp.wrcc.dri.edu/nps/photodocumentation.pdf. (accessed 15 August 2004)

Redmond, K. T. and D. B. Simeral. 2004. Climate monitoring comments: Central Alaska Network Inventory and Monitoring Program. Available from ftp://ftp.wrcc.dri.edu/nps/alaska/cakn/npscakncomments040406.pdf. (accessed 6 April 2004)

Redmond, K. T., D. B. Simeral, and G. D. McCurdy. 2005. Climate monitoring for southwest Alaska national parks: network design and site selection. Report 05-01. Western Regional Climate Center, Reno, Nevada.

Redmond, K. T., and G. D. McCurdy. 2005. Channel Islands National Park: Design considerations for weather and climate monitoring. Report 05-02. Western Regional Climate Center, Reno, Nevada.

Sevruk, B., and W. R. Hamon. 1984. International comparison of national precipitation gauges with a reference pit gauge. Instruments and Observing Methods, Report No 17, WMO/TD – 38, World Meteorological Organization, Geneva, Switzerland.

Simpson, J. J., Hufford, G. L., C. Daly, J. S. Berg, and M. D. Fleming. 2005. Comparing maps of mean monthly surface temperature and precipitation for Alaska and adjacent areas of Canada produced by two different methods. Arctic **58**:137-161.

Whiteman, C. D. 2000. Mountain Meteorology: Fundamentals and Applications. Oxford University Press, Oxford, UK.

Wilson, E. O. 1998. Consilience: The Unity of Knowledge. Knopf, New York.

World Meteorological Organization. 1983. Guide to meteorological instruments and methods of observation, No. 8, 5th edition, World Meteorological Organization, Geneva Switzerland.

World Meteorological Organization. 2005. Organization and planning of intercomparisons of rainfall intensity gauges. World Meteorological Organization, Geneva Switzerland.

Yang, D., B. E. Goodison, J. R. Metcalfe, V. S. Golubev, R. Bates, T. Pangburn, and C. Hanson. 1998. Accuracy of NWS 8" standard nonrecording precipitation gauge: results and application of WMO intercomparison. Journal of Atmospheric and Oceanic Technology **15**:54-68.

Yang, D., B. E. Goodison, J. R. Metcalfe, P. Louie, E. Elomaa, C. Hanson, V. Bolubev, T. Gunther, J. Milkovic, and M. Lapin. 2001. Compatibility evaluation of national precipitation gauge measurements. Journal of Geophysical Research **106**:1481-1491.

Appendix F. Descriptions of weather/climate monitoring networks.

F.1. Clean Air Status and Trends Network (CASTNet)

- Purpose of network: provide information for evaluating the effectiveness of national emission-control strategies.
- Primary management agency: EPA.
- Data website: http://epa.gov/castnet/.
- Measured weather/climate elements:
  o Air temperature.
  o Precipitation.
  o Relative humidity.
  o Wind speed.
  o Wind direction.
  o Wind gust.
  o Gust direction.
  o Solar radiation.
  o Soil moisture and temperature.
- Sampling frequency: hourly.
- Reporting frequency: hourly.
- Estimated station cost: $13K.
- Network strengths:
  o High-quality data.
  o Sites are well maintained.
- Network weaknesses:
  o Density of station coverage is low.
  o Shorter periods of record for western United States.

CASTNet primarily is an air-quality-monitoring network managed by the EPA. The elements shown here are intended to support interpretation of measured air-quality parameters such as ozone, nitrates, sulfides, etc., which also are measured at CASTNet sites.

F.2. NWS Cooperative Observer Program (COOP)

- Purpose of network:
  o Provide observational, meteorological data required to define U.S. climate and help measure long-term climate changes.
  o Provide observational, meteorological data in near real-time to support forecasting and warning mechanisms and other public service programs of the NWS.
- Primary management agency: NOAA (NWS).
- Data website: data are available from the NCDC (http://www.ncdc.noaa.gov), RCCs (e.g., WRCC, http://www.wrcc.dri.edu), and state climate offices.
- Measured weather/climate elements
  o Maximum, minimum, and observation-time temperature.
  o Precipitation, snowfall, snow depth.

- o Pan evaporation (some stations).
- Sampling frequency: daily.
- Reporting frequency: daily or monthly (station-dependent).
- Estimated station cost: $2K with maintenance costs of $500–900/year.
- Network strengths:
  - o Decade–century records at most sites.
  - o Widespread national coverage (thousands of stations).
  - o Excellent data quality when well maintained.
  - o Relatively inexpensive; highly cost effective.
  - o Manual measurements; not automated.
- Network weaknesses:
  - o Uneven exposures; many are not well-maintained.
  - o Dependence on schedules for volunteer observers.
  - o Slow entry of data from many stations into national archives.
  - o Data subject to observational methodology; not always documented.
  - o Manual measurements; not automated and not hourly.

The COOP network has long served as the main climate observation network in the United States. Readings are usually made by volunteers using equipment supplied, installed, and maintained by the federal government. The observer in effect acts as a host for the data-gathering activities and supplies the labor; this is truly a "cooperative" effort. The SAO sites often are considered to be part of the cooperative network as well if they collect the previously mentioned types of weather/climate observations. Typical observation days are morning to morning, evening to evening, or midnight to midnight. By convention, observations are ascribed to the date the instrument was reset at the end of the observational period. For this reason, midnight observations represent the end of a day. The Historical Climate Network is a subset of the cooperative network but contains longer and more complete records.

F.3. Remote Automated Weather Station (RAWS)

- Purpose of network: provide near-real-time (hourly or near hourly) measurements of meteorological variables for use in fire weather forecasts and climatology. Data from RAWS also are used for natural resource management, flood forecasting, natural hazard management, and air-quality monitoring.
- Primary management agency: WRCC, National Interagency Fire Center.
- Data website: http://www.raws.dri.edu/index.html.
- Measured weather/climate elements:
  - o Air temperature.
  - o Precipitation.
  - o Relative humidity.
  - o Wind speed.
  - o Wind direction.
  - o Wind gust.
  - o Gust direction.
  - o Solar radiation.
  - o Soil moisture and temperature.

- Sampling frequency: 1 or 10 minutes, element-dependent.
- Reporting frequency: generally hourly. Some stations report every 15 or 30 minutes.
- Estimated station cost: $12K with satellite telemetry ($8K without satellite telemetry); maintenance costs are around $2K/year.
- Network strengths:
  o Metadata records are usually complete.
  o Sites are located in remote areas.
  o Sites are generally well-maintained.
  o Entire period of record available on-line.
- Network weaknesses:
  o RAWS network is focused largely on fire management needs (formerly focused only on fire needs).
  o Frozen precipitation is not measured reliably.
  o Station operation is not always continuous.
  o Data transmission is completed via one-way telemetry. Data are therefore recoverable either in real-time or not at all.

The RAWS network is used by many land-management agencies, such as the BLM, NPS, Fish and Wildlife Service, Bureau of Indian Affairs, Forest Service, and other agencies. The RAWS network was one of the first automated weather station networks to be installed in the United States. Most gauges do not have heaters, so hydrologic measurements are of little value when temperatures dip below freezing or reach freezing after frozen precipitation events. There are approximately 1100 real-time sites in this network and about 1800 historic sites (some are decommissioned or moved). The sites can transmit data all winter but may be in deep snow in some locations. The WRCC is the archive for this network and receives station data and metadata through a special connection to the National Interagency Fire Center in Boise, Idaho.

F.4. NWS Surface Airways Observation Program (SAO)

- Purpose of network: provide near-real-time (hourly or near hourly) measurements of meteorological variables and are used both for airport operations and weather forecasting.
- Primary management agency: NOAA, FAA.
- Data website: data are available from state climate offices, RCCs (e.g., WRCC, http://www.wrcc.dri.edu), and NCDC (http://www.ncdc.noaa.gov).
- Measured weather/climate elements:
  o Air temperature.
  o Dewpoint and/or relative humidity.
  o Wind speed.
  o Wind direction.
  o Wind gust.
  o Gust direction.
  o Barometric pressure.
  o Precipitation (not at many FAA sites).
  o Sky cover.
  o Ceiling (cloud height).
  o Visibility.

- Sampling frequency: element-dependent.
- Reporting frequency: element-dependent.
- Estimated station cost: $100–$200K with maintenance costs approximately $10K/year.
- Network strengths:
  o Records generally extend over several decades.
  o Consistent maintenance and station operations.
  o Data record is reasonably complete and usually high quality.
  o Hourly or sub-hourly data.
- Network weaknesses:
  o Nearly all sites are located at airports.
  o Data quality can be related to size of airport—smaller airports tend to have poorer datasets.
  o Influences from urbanization and other land-use changes.

These stations are managed by NOAA, U. S. Navy, U. S. Air Force, and FAA. These stations are located generally at major airports and military bases. The FAA stations often do not record precipitation, or they may provide precipitation records of reduced quality. Automated stations are typically ASOSs for the NWS or AWOSs for the FAA. Some sites only report episodically with observers paid per observation.

Appendix G. Electronic supplements.

G.1. ACIS metadata file for weather and climate stations associated with the ERMN:
http://www.wrcc.dri.edu/nps/pub/ermn/metadata/ERMN_from_ACIS.tar.gz.

G.2. ERMN metadata files for weather and climate stations associated with the ERMN:
http://www.wrcc.dri.edu/nps/pub/ermn/metadata/ERMN_NPS.tar.gz.

NPS/ERMN/NRTR—2006/006, September 2006